D0040229

A SAN FRANCISCO CONSERVATIVE

David Parker Essays

Volume Two

Waterside Productions
2055 Oxford Ave
Cardiff, CA 92007
www.waterside.com

Copyright © 2022 by David Parker
www.davidparkeressays.com

All rights reserved. This book or any portion thereof may not be
reproduced or used in any manner whatsoever without the express written
permission of the publisher except for the use of brief quotations in articles
and book reviews.

Printed in the United States of America

ISBN-13: 978-1-956503-06-7 print edition
ISBN-13: 978-1-956503-07-4 ebook edition

The author would like to thank the following publishers for their
permission to reprint:

Excerpts from *Witness* by Whittaker Chambers. Copyright © 1952 by
Whittaker Chambers. Reprinted by permission of Regnery History and
Regnery Publishing.

Excerpts from *The Black Book of the American Left: The Collected
Conservative Writings of David Horowitz* by David Horowitz. Copyright ©
2017 by David Horowitz. Reprinted by permission of Encounter Books.

Excerpts from *The Death and Life of Great American Cities* by Jane
Jacobs, copyright © 1961, 1989 by Jane Jacobs. Used by permission of
Random House, an imprint and division of Penguin Random House LLC.
All rights reserved.

Gary Snyder, "Things to Do Around San Francisco" from *Mountains and
Rivers Without End*. Copyright © 1996, 2013 by Gary Snyder. Reprinted
with the permission of The Permissions Company, LLC on behalf of
Counterpoint Press, counterpointpress.com

"After the Cries of the Birds" by Lawrence Ferlinghetti, from *The Secret
Meaning of Things*, copyright © 1968 by Lawrence Ferlinghetti. Reprinted
by permission of New Directions Publishing Corp.

DEDICATION

To John Diamante, my editor for so many years that I realize now that it is to you that I am writing.

Time present and time past
Are both perhaps contained in time future,
And time future contained in time past.

—T.S. Eliot, *Four Quartets*

CONTENTS

4. SELECTED WRITINGS

INTRODUCTION

I have 150 years' personal experience. That's why I write: to tell progressives what I know.

I know, for example, the opening quote by T.S. Eliot is the absolute purest statement of classical conservatism: time past, time present, time future, they're the same, which is why people and nations should reform, not change, basics. Conservatism means conserve. Human beings, their centuries-old institutions, nature, the universe, evolution—all, are the result of trial-and-error, all, have an element of perfection, none, are a product of design. Society and culture are not products of design. No species in nature plan their society. The queen bee does not tell other bees what to do. Bees know what to do. And we humans know what to do: behavior and morality are encoded in our genes.

> There is no need to try to live in harmony with nature; you can't live any other way.
>
> —Friedrich Nietzsche, *Genealogy of Morals*

> *Wu wei er wu bu wei*. In essence, "Do nothing and everything will be accomplished."
>
> —Lao Tzu, 6th century BC

To leaders of warring states, Lao Tzu advised: stop fighting each other, give your people a break, give them a little freedom and they'll work out all your problems. Do nothing, and everything will be accomplished.

> And as Machiavelli maintained, give the people some economic freedom. They will be so grateful they will support you when you need them. Do not rely on the aristocracy; they are vain and disloyal.
>
> —Machiavelli, The *Prince,* 1580 [The root of modern democracy.]

Do nothing? People will die. No, they won't. Don't underestimate human beings. Consider a homeless person lying on the sidewalk. A progressive's first response is to phone city services to pick him up: A, B, C, D. A progressive, A, sees a problem (for example, a homeless person), B, and tells government, C, to take taxpayers', D, money and give it to B. "A" is in the habit of telling "D," government, to take care of things because he knows himself too well, knows that since *he* isn't going to help that homeless person, no one else may either. *That's* why progressives want big government: to ease their conscience.

A conservative's first response is to bend over and ask that person if he needs help, call for help, wait until it arrives, later, donate to the charity that sent the ambulance. (This San Francisco conservative speaks from experience.) Conservatives detest the idea of citizens delegating personal responsibility to government. Not afraid of freedom, of democracy (constitutional democracy), conservatives see almost no need for government. Jeffersonians, conservatives believe individuals can be counted on to do the right thing.

1

CONSERVATISM

Anarchy, State and Utopia

Society must incorporate a few universal values. Pluralism is such a value, namely, different groups of people living together—with sometimes one group in power (through election), later, others. But when one group's identity is elevated above pluralism, democracy is subverted. The more that one side says only their view counts, the closer we are to tyranny.[1]

In America, the loss of pluralism is most dangerous in the nation's schools and universities where "woke" liberals, considering their opinions quasi-sacred, their critics oh-so-wrong, use their concentrated power of students and professors to dictate what may be said and who may speak on campus. To such liberals, speech cannot be divorced from the identity of the speaker—why conservative speech is censored. Should conservatives argue that patriarchy and white privilege are not a fact or that gender norms are purely arbitrary, liberals go ballistic. True or false, what's relevant is

---

[1] Observe liberal activists at universities overturning tables where conservatives are handing out leaflets. Those light brown cancel culture boots are on their way to lockstep dark brown boots. UC Berkeley.

3

that speech in America must not be censored. Since the 1970s, thousands of teachers, professors and administrators have lost their positions (or were never hired) simply for tolerating conservatism. The American anti-fascist campaign to eliminate conservatives from education has been successful.[2]

Liberals who sideline or step upon the principles that created this nation should read John Locke's *2nd Treatise on Civil Government*:

> [Individuals] are in a state of perfect freedom to order their actions and dispose of their possessions and persons, as they think fit . . . without asking leave, or dependency upon the will of any other man. [Section 4]

> [The bounds of the laws of nature require that] no one ought to harm another in his life, health, liberty or possessions. [Section 6]

> All men may be restrained from invading others rights, and from doing hurt to one another. Everyone has the right to punish the transgressor (proportionate to the transgression). [Section 7 and 8][3]

––––––––––

A nation's government must not *use* individuals to solve social problems, for example, tax individuals to redistribute wealth. "Individuals are ends, not means to an end. They may not be sacrificed for achieving ends to which they do not consent." – Immanuel Kant.

There are no species in nature where leaders tell others what to do. Let that be humanity's guide: the spontaneity of the invisible hand of nature that created everything we have—language, custom, money, common law built over centuries, a trading economy. Crime, too, is a product of evolution and should therefore be dealt with

---

[2] 1.5 percent of college faculties are conservative. See David Brooks, Chapter 3, footnote 73.

[3] John Locke, *2nd Treatise on Civil Government* (Pantianos Classics, first published in 1689; still in print).

naturally, wherein a natural desire for justice is satisfied through immediate punishment (not years later when the perpetrator is no longer the same person). In *Anarchy, State and Utopia*, Robert Nozick elaborates on a cost-benefit analysis to determine the extent of law enforcement, the extent of retribution. It was not necessary. Necessary is to impose a few rules about which a society has achieved consensus: the U.S. Constitution, one page; the Bill of Rights, one page; the Ten Commandments, one page—and enforce them. Purposely drop a candy wrapper on the sidewalk: prison—one hour.

Don't underestimate human beings. An evolved species, citizens understood New York City Mayor Rudy Giuliani (who drastically reduced crime): zero tolerance, punish *all* crimes. People got the message. Our Jeffersonian democracy is based on the notion that citizens can and do think for themselves. Our Lockean democracy is based on the notion that the sole purpose of government is to protect the life, liberty and property of free and independent citizens. To Nozick, anything less ignores the right of persons to give what they produce to whomever they choose.[4] To this author, attacking producers ignores the fact that the most important participants in a market economy are its producers, individuals who (along with labor), must not be forced to give away their hours or work extra hours to pay for services they're not asking for, government-mandated health insurance, for example. To Nozick,

---

[4] What people create—their art, inventions, crops, the land upon which those crops were cultivated (and by extension, additional land purchased by selling their creations)—*that* is property. Although stolen land should be returned, economic reality is that, in America, land ownership today is exactly how it would be if land had not been stolen. Lacking the entrepreneurial vision of those who followed, past owners would have sold their land for what would have seemed to them an irresistible price, multiples of what they deemed it was worth. (In Southern California, visionaries William Mulholland, Henry Huntington, and Charles Crocker did exactly that—in the 1920s, '30s and '40s, they bought all the land between Owens Valley and Los Angeles. In the 1980s and '90s in New York City, Donald Trump purchased buildings at astonishingly high prices, Trump Tower at Columbus Park Circle, for instance, where he may have paid $1 million for units worth $500,000 that are today worth $10 million.) Land ownership would be the same today even if, in the 1930s, the nation had turned Communist. Why? Because communism, false theory, collapses. Redistributed wealth wears out, production slows, citizens are forced to return to some form of market capitalism as in Russia, China, Vietnam. Cuba can't wait. In Communist nations there is no incentive to produce, so no one produces. (Continued on next page)

5

the moral argument is that the state has no right to compel citizens who are not asking the state for anything.[5] Forcing citizens is not a basis for building community.[6]

———————

Theories of distributive justice show disbelief in the market process. Yet, trickle-down theory *is* how an economy works: producers create the economy, workers are glad to have a job. Every economy has hardships, but in a market economy they are offset by a far greater good in the aggregate. The poor in a socialist economy think they are well off because they're not aware they are poor: everyone is poor. In a rich nation, they notice. In America they notice because the poor are poor in relation to the wealthy.

But the poor in America are not poor in absolute terms; they live better than 95 percent of the rest of the world.[7] For the last 400 years, those wishing to better their lives have moved here, not the

———————

(Continued from previous page) "To each according to his needs, from each according to his ability" (Marxism) *guarantees* that citizens show need, not ability. Consider Plymouth Rock under Governor William Bradford, 1620. To ensure equality, colonists were given equal portions of land, then, forbidden to sell or pay others to work it. Those capable of producing twice as much from the same parcel were forbidden to farm other parcels. Those possessing other talents, not interested in farming, were forced to farm. [Life in the Soviet Union.] Entrepreneurial colonists simply jumped the fence and farmed outside the fort—a perfect example of how markets circumvent regulation. Bradford canceled his equality rule.

In other words, governments have no business telling citizens what to do. Academe bureaucrats, believing such nonsense as "resources are scarce," have no right to tell others where to live or what and how much to consume. Resources aren't scarce. The earth is *huge*. Land is not scarce. At one-half acre per person, the entire population of the U.S. fits into the state of Texas. Water is not scarce. The Amazon River dumps 7.381 million cubic feet of fresh water *per second* into the Atlantic Ocean. Oil is not scarce. There are at least 90 billion barrels of oil under the Arctic, 264 billion barrels in the U.S., 168 billion barrels in Canada, 800 billion barrels of oil in the Middle East. Abundant energy? Nuclear.

[5] Robert Nozick, *Anarchy, State and Utopia* (Basic Books, 1974), p. 168.

[6] Nozick, p. 174. Forced bussing to integrate public schools and forced affirmative action to integrate employment and university admittance do not engender fraternity. Voluntary bussing, voluntary affirmative action, that does.

[7] With hot and cold running water, heat and air-conditioning, inexpensive food, dwellings built to high safety standards, public transportation, public education, health care, Social Security.

other way around. In 1790, the U.S. population was 4 million. In 1990, 250 million; in 2020, 330 million. After China and India, America today, with twice the population of Japan, is the third largest nation in the world. In the forefronts of science, technology, business, and the arts, America's high standard of living reflects the opportunistic intelligence of a *self-selected* immigrant population (unlike the rest of the world whose citizens are born and remain where they were born).

European socialism? The poor in Europe receive more benefits than the poor in America, but must live in a highly regulated uncreative business environment, where workers, rather than dream of work, dream of early retirement (in France, at age 55 if you work for the nationalized railroad). Except that in socialist economies, large portions of the population are always unemployed. Government make-work is not work; collecting unemployment insurance is not employment. During the 2008 economic downturn, 25 percent of the workforce in semi-socialist France was unemployed. During the 2013 recovery, 10 to 15 percent. Unemployment in the U.S. was 9 and 3 percent, respectively.

One very strange liberal notion connected with distributive justice is that the wealthy should be allowed to keep all the money they need (to lead their wealthy life), but beyond that amount forfeit the rest to the state to give to the less fortunate.

Another strange liberal notion is that the wealthy, because they live in a society where tax dollars contribute to the infrastructure that make it possible for them to become rich, have a duty to see that no one lives in poverty. Both are complete nonsense. In 1965, poverty in America was 15 percent of the population. The War on Poverty was the liberal solution—except that 55 years and 23 trillion dollars in U.S. government debt later, poverty is still 15 percent, *as it remained*, on average, through those 55 years.[8]

Politicians asked for that War on Poverty, and politicians still ask for funds—for infrastructure, research and development, public

---

[8] United States Census Bureau, *Historical Poverty Tables: People and Families—1959 to 2019*, https://www.census.gov/data/tables/time-series/demo/income-poverty/historical-poverty-people.html.

transportation, the damming of every river in America. People in business are not asking for that. Politicians ask because delivering on such promises gets them reelected: throwing money at problems without explaining to middle-class voters that it is *they*, not the rich, who pay.[9]

Successful countries are the result of their entrepreneurs. Producers in a supply-side economy must therefore be protected: they are the ones at risk. If not confident, they will *not* invest. If regulated, or if government pumps money into the economy, they will *not* operate. They know that money is temporary, that consumers will hoard it in preparation for the pump running dry, the Ricardian equivalence (or, if you're a Keynesian, the liquidity trap). Producers know that such basics as infrastructure, rule of law, private ownership of property, come *afterward*. Governments think they come first, that nations are poor because governments haven't provided those basics, precisely why foreign and domestic aid fails: *initiative must come from the entrepreneur, not the donor*. Aid must go to entrepreneurial individuals, not their governments. Plus, to receive aid is to break a basic rule in starting a business: don't borrow. Grow your business, reinvest profit. Borrowing is for professional investors, not for those trying to better their lives.

> The illegitimate use of a state by economic interests for their own ends is based upon a preexisting illegitimate power of the state to enrich some persons at the expense of others. Eliminate that illegitimate power of giving differential economic benefits and you eliminate or drastically reduce the motive for wanting political influence.[10]

To end corruption in government, end government. Create a minimal state that protects—a night watchman. The United Nations could be that institution worldwide, except the UN can't even stop small nations from fighting—why this author says, "Nations of the

---

[9] You can't tax the poor, they can't pay; you can't tax the rich, they won't pay; you can only tax the middle class, they have no idea how to get out of it.

[10] Nozick, *Anarchy, State and Utopia*, p. 272.

world, stop trying to solve your problems through the political process. Life doesn't work that way: outside of socialism, the political process cannot solve economic problems. Economic problems are personal; governments, impersonal. Governments cannot solve their citizens' personal problems by redistributing the earnings of richer citizens. Those richer citizens will leave—after sending their money offshore."[11]

Rich or poor, citizens do not want their earnings going into the pockets of politicians, populists elected by telling voters they will get tax money spent in *their* district, asking voters, "Why are you not benefiting from government largesse? Is it because you earn $100 a month more than those who do?" Always, the argument is that the cutoff line is arbitrary.

What's not understood is that socialism only works in rich nations—nations rich enough to afford the social, political, and economic waste from redistributing middle-class earnings (even if in the form of goods and services the middle class would have purchased anyway: health care, child care, education, pensions). Politicizing social and economic problems, allowing social programs to remove the necessity of individual responsibility, only rich nations can afford the interest on the debt that pays for such waste.

————————

Utopia doesn't mean perfection: it means *your* vision of the best of all possible worlds. Progressives have no monopoly on such a vision. Pluralist societies will always include some citizens whose vision is "no government," who acknowledge de Tocqueville's appreciation of America (1835) as a land where individuals take responsibility for their lives.

In "Politics," Aristotle said there is a choice: a communal society where no one owns property, a mixed society where there is some ownership of property, or a free society where all property is

---

[11] The first thing Donald Trump did as president was lower the corporate tax rate. Yet he also ordered American corporations, Apple, for example, headquartered in Ireland, to repatriate their cash.

privately owned. He chose a free society because that's the only society that guarantees diversity. Yes, Aristotle's words.[12]

What if citizens vote to have a socialist society? Let them, but make certain they first experiment in one small region, not the entire nation—unlike the French and Bolshevik Revolutions, which forced everyone to conform to *their* particular vision or die. That's totalitarianism, socialism's logical outcome—because taking property by force (even if purchased) is illegal, and citizens will revolt, after which the state will crush them. America doesn't confiscate private property, but not because America is a democracy, a nation where the majority rules, but because America is a constitutional democracy, a nation where laws rule, not men. Citizens cannot vote 90 to 10 to take private property. It's *unconstitutional*.

As long as citizens can escape to a state respectful of their larger (or smaller) vision of freedom and diversity, socialism cannot thrive: citizens simply compare free-market states to socialist states (West Germany to East Germany), then abandon the socialist model. Nations can't live half-free, half-slave. Citizens cannot impose their vision on a constitutionally based government; government cannot impose its vision on a constitutionally free citizenry—force them to purchase health insurance, for example, or to hire minorities. That's Dystopia.

An ideal society allows for some bad behavior: its latitude makes its people better. De Tocqueville commented that only by being free [to make mistakes] can people develop virtues [integrity], capabilities and responsibilities. In socialist societies, everything is done for you. Your teacher does your homework. What's the point? Better, a minimal state where citizens depend on each other, deal

---

[12] *The Philosophy of Aristotle (with commentary by Renford Bambrough)* (Mentor Books, 1963), "Politics," Book II, Section 5, pp. 392-399. College students, before you advocate anything, read something modern, such as Aristotle. Our Founding Fathers did. Rising to the occasion, diversity *was* their vision—give maximum freedom to the states so that dissatisfied citizens have a choice as to where to live. Not possible when a centralized government controls the nation. Nozick, in *Anarchy, State and Utopia,* recommends that students also read Shakespeare, Tolstoy, Jane Austen, Rabelais and Dostoyevsky—to remind themselves just how different people are.

with each other, inevitably respect each other—the only cure for racism and ethnic hatred.

The goal: independent citizens living in a minimal state, free to say and do what they please within an agreed upon set of rules. Independent, responsible, investing their capital so that when they retire, they will be financially independent: that's Utopia!

Conservatism

> The conservative temperament is an acknowledged feature of human society everywhere.
>
> —Sir Roger Scruton[13]

Everywhere and throughout history, classical liberalism, conservatism, reason: Apollo. Romantic liberalism, progressivism, emotion: Dionysus.

> Conservatism starts from a sentiment that all mature people can readily share: the sentiment that good things are easily destroyed, but not easily created. This is especially true of the good things that come to us as collective assets: peace, freedom, law, civility, public spirit, the security of property and family life, in all of which we depend on the cooperation of others while having no means single-handedly to obtain it. In respect of such things, the work of destruction is quick, easy and exhilarating; the work of creation slow, laborious and dull. That is one of the lessons of the 20th century. It is also one reason why conservatives suffer such a disadvantage when it comes to public opinion. Their position is true but boring, that of their opponent exciting but false.
>
> —Sir Roger Scruton[14]

---

[13] Roger Scruton, *How to be a Conservative* (Bloomsbury Publishing, 2014), p. *vii*.

[14] Scruton, p. *viii*.

British and American common law, built over centuries, parliaments, due process, *habeas corpus* (the state cannot hold you without immediate trial), our long history of democracy, today, among progressives, is taken for granted, is not always defended properly (in the opinions of Supreme Court Justices Antonin Scalia and Clarence Thomas), as society sticks less and less to principles, to the U.S. Constitution, to the masterpiece in its defense, *The Federalist Papers*, because, when compared to contemporary social and economic injustices, those principles are just too difficult to uphold. Because to progressives, the U.S. Constitution is a living document whose meaning is not fixed.[15]

It is *that* interpretation of the Constitution that allows liberalism today to focus on issues rather than principles. It is *that* interpretation that allowed President Barack Obama to declare, "I detest ideologues, Left and Right; I am a pragmatist. It is more important to get something done, the Affordable Care Act, for example, than just leave things as they are."[16] However, such a halfway solution puts the nation in a halfway position: half socialist, half free—why the problem of the high cost of health care will never be solved. The Affordable Care Act insured those who were uninsured, but the Act was not designed to lower the price of health care. Understood was that price would rise in the long run, be paid for by borrowing (like Medicare and Social Security) and that the Act was yet another attempt to create universal health care. Except, the first attempt, Medicare, extended health care so far beyond market demand that price tripled. Before Medicare, 1965, the price of health insurance was the price of auto insurance, property

---

[15] The U.S. Constitution is *one* page (on large parchment). The Ten Commandments, ten sentences. A society that can't stick to a few simple rules has no chance. Europe wants no part. European socialists have moved forward from that pinnacle. The EU Constitution, 254 pages, expands, not limits government power. Rather than adhere to common law and constitutional principles built over centuries, believing that every case must be judged on its merit, not simply referred to a holding, the EU (like Congress) writes law every day. That's "progressivism," belief that there is nothing to learn from the past because every situation is different. Britain should never have joined such a union, thus, Brexit.

[16] Conversation between Barack Obama and John McCain during the 2008 presidential campaign, as recalled by this author.

insurance, life insurance, about $200 a month (in 2020 dollars)—a price everyone can afford. Unless the free market for health care is brought back, price will never drop. Cancel Medicare.

————————

> When the chips are down, [British] workers do not defend their class but their country, and they associate their country with a gentle way of life in which unusual and eccentric habits—such as not killing one another—are accepted as the way things are. In these respects, Orwell [a Leftist] also thought that leftist intellectuals will always misunderstand the workers, who want nothing to do with a self-vaunting [woke] disloyalty that only intellectuals can afford.[17]

> —Sir Roger Scruton[18]

Beware destruction of what has stood the test of time, of what is difficult to reproduce. Arnold Schoenberg's music, atonal, was not designed to replace the great tradition of German music—but prolong it. To Schoenberg, because German music had lapsed into cliché and kitsch, it was necessary to purify the dialect of tribes (German 18th- and 19th-century composers). To Scruton, "[W]e must be modern in defense of the past and creative in defense of tradition."[19]

Opposite are the French, Bolshevik, and Cuban Revolutions: modern in defense of the future, creative in defense of the unknown. Marx declared repeatedly that communism is so new that no one

-----

[17] As Islam elevates religion above nationality as a test of membership, Islam poses a threat to world political order, certainly to Western civilization. As woke liberals elevate political correctness above nationality, and rights of community and state above those of the individual, above the ideas of the Age of Enlightenment—classical liberalism upon which this nation was founded—calling such ideas the philosophy of white, misogynous, slave-holding, class-privileged males, so, too, do woke liberals pose a threat to world order.

[18] Scruton, *How to be a Conservative*, p. 3. George Orwell, *Essays*, (Everyman's Library, 2002), *The Lion and the Unicorn: Socialism and the English Genius* (Reading Essentials, 1941), pp. 291-348.

[19] Scruton, *How to be a Conservative*, p. 4.

knows how it will work, that we just have to try it.[20] Except, why wasn't communism tried first on a small region? Why was it imposed on whole nations, whole continents? Because romantic Dionysian Marxists knew in their hearts they were right, that the world would thank them later, would consider the 60 million Russians, Chinese, Cambodians, Cubans, and North Koreans deliberately executed as a small price to pay for a long-term future of mankind finally rid of bourgeois ownership of the means of production, finally rid of capitalism.

The slow accumulation of law, law stemming from individual cases brought before courts since the 13th century, common law, has stood the test of time—a valuable product of British and American history. It is not, according to woke progressives, a weapon of the ruling class.

> [This] desire to control society in the name of equality expresses the contempt for human freedom.
>
> [That is] the impertinence of a political party that sets out to confiscate whole industries from those who had created them, to abolish [independent public] schools [by amalgamating them], to control relations in the workplace, to regulate hours of work, to compel workers to join a union, to ban hunting [in Britain] to take property from a landlord and bestow it on his tenant [rent control], to compel businesses to sell themselves to the government at a dictated price, to police all activities through [self-appointed vigilantes] designed to check for political correctness.
>
> —Sir Roger Scruton[21]

---

[20] "We just have to try it!" is what Speaker Nancy Pelosi said about the Affordable Care Act before it was approved by Congress and the Supreme Court. "It's going to be very, very exciting. [Congress has] to pass the bill so that you can find out what is in it, away from the fog of controversy." Nancy Pelosi, Interview broadcast on CNN's State of the Union (cited by *The Washington Times, September 22, 2013*).

[21] Scruton, *How to be a Conservative*, p. 12.

The essence of conservatism, T. S. Eliot's idea that time past, present and future are the same, has its roots in the father of conservatism, Edmund Burke, who, commenting on the French Revolution as it was unfolding, 1789,[22] warned Britain not to do such a thing, not to trash its past, the intentions of those now dead who bestowed trusts and endowments, not, as in the French self-made emergency, to exchange the idea of reform for the creation of something new. Burke warned not to let the emotional French terrorist mob be an example for Britain, a mob not listening to reason, for example, that the young king and queen (Marie Antoinette), teenagers, were willing to share power; that the National Assembly was willing to transition to a constitutional democracy; that the jailor who guarded the Bastille (someone who genuinely cared for his prisoners) should not have been indiscriminately murdered.

A product of its zealousness, ostensibly to transfer power from the top—monarchy, landed aristocracy, Catholic Church—to citizens below, the French Revolution transferred power to a new top —a dictatorship of the charismatic terrorist Robespierre, and ten years later, to Napoleon.

To paraphrase Scruton, the Revolution was a violent disruption to society's historical development, to interpersonal relations among family, workplace, church and schools, where people learn responsibility for their actions. The Revolution turned to organization from the top, to government, where accountability disappears as government breeds "progressive" individuals who think in terms of regulation and taxation.[23]

To conservatives, the notion that governments are instituted to regulate citizens' lives is absurd; the notion of nonpartisan elites working together à la Woodrow Wilson progressivism to make the world a better place is absurd. There are progressives who would agree. In *The World of Yesterday*, Stephen Zweig attributes the decline of civil order in Europe [1930s] to the myth of progress—

---

[22] Edmund Burke, *Reflections on the Revolution in France* (1790).

[23] Scruton, *How to be a Conservative,* p. 21.

why Scruton believes that in all the ideologies of the day, communism, socialism, Nazism, fascism, Zweig saw the same pernicious attempt to rewrite the principles of social order in terms of a linear progression [progressivism] from past to future. The cult of the leader, the "vanguard party," the "avant-garde," all supposed that society has a direction—in the way that business has a purpose and armies have a goal—why those leaders felt they had the right to conscript all citizens into the machinery of the state.[24]

People can disagree. In a family, people can disagree because they still share an identity. In politics, citizens can disagree if they share an identity, a "national we." Without that identity they can't live together. In Britain and America, that identity is our history of freedom and democracy, our willingness to abide by a few rules, a constitution. The U.S. has 50 states with a common identity. The EU has 50 states without common identity. Created to prevent another

---

[24] Stefan Zweig, *Die Welt von Gestern* (*The World of Yesterday*) (Viking, 1943), in Scruton, p. 27.

Franklin D. Roosevelt was deeply impressed by what Mussolini had accomplished, and in return, in a laudatory review of Roosevelt's 1933 book, *Looking Forward*, Mussolini wrote, "Reminiscent of Fascism is the principle that the state no longer leaves the economy to its own devices . . . Without question, the mood accompanying this sea change resembles that of Fascism." At the time, the chief Nazi newspaper, *Völkischer Beobachter*, repeatedly praised "Roosevelt's adoption of National Socialist strains of thought in his economic and social policies" and "the development toward an authoritarian state" based on the "demand that collective good be put before individual self-interest." With respect to the Great Depression, Roosevelt declared, "[I]f we are to go forward, we must move as a trained and loyal army willing to sacrifice for the good of a common discipline. We are, I know, ready and willing to submit our lives and property to such discipline, because it makes possible a leadership which aims at a larger good. I assume unhesitantly the leadership of this great army . . . I shall ask the Congress for the one remaining instrument to meet the crisis—broad Executive power to wage a war against the emergency, as great as the power that would be given to me if we were in fact invaded by a foreign foe." For the above quotes, see David Boaz, "Hitler, Mussolini, Roosevelt," *Reason* magazine, October 2007, a review of German cultural historian Wolfgang Schivelbusch's book, *Three New Deals: Reflections on Roosevelt's America, Mussolini's Italy, and Hitler's Germany, 1933-1939*.

Compare:
> If I am to build unity among the people, I must first find a new front, a common enemy so that everyone knows: We must be united, because this enemy is the enemy of us all. If we are not united, the entire German people will sink into the abyss.
> —Nuremberg Rally,1927, Adolf Hitler

World War, the EU, like its weak model the UN, cannot handle the unbridled nationalism currently tearing it apart. Unbridled populism is the reason Yugoslavia, Syria, Somalia, and Nigeria fell apart. According to Scruton, lacking national sovereignty, they could not adapt to changing conditions.[25]

The conservative temperament has its roots in classical liberalism, in social, political and economic freedom—in not censoring human action. *Modern* liberalism, progressivism, the opposite, has its roots in curing social and economic injustice by restraining social, political and economic freedom—a most unJeffersonian fear of the economy and democracy, a fear that the wealthy are rich at the expense of the poor. That zero-sum Marxist fallacy underlies the progressive notion that equality and justice are the same thing, the default position of socialism programmed today into almost all university courses on political economy.

Except not everyone believes that Jack having more money than Jill is a sign of injustice. If Jack belongs to a *class* with money, and Jill to a class without money, zero-sum kicks in, because people are persuaded that Jack became rich at the expense of Jill: Marxism behind today's social reforms—that the poor performance of the nation's public schools and its police departments is a product of racism and class privilege. With their "cultural revolution," today's woke Marxists would defund the police and retrain all teachers.

Progressivism refuses to accept that inequality is a phenomenon of nature, that people are different, have different values, that even making honest effort is not a universal value, although in America it is, why immigrants come here: to flee places where effort is not universal, where there is no opportunity to better their lives, why, within two generations, despite ethnic or racial discrimination, immigrants in America succeed. They turn to their

---

[25] Scruton, *How to be a Conservative,* p. 33.

own community. They do not, as do African-Americans, turn to the political process to force those outside their community to hire them. A huge mistake—because in a free nation, the political process is not capable of solving economic or social problems.

Disparity between rich and poor in America is not, however, as great as it seems. Today's economy, shifting to the digital age, leaves some behind (temporarily) while others become wealthy (temporarily), but in 30 years, that will even out.

Governments must stop trying to correct for injustice; it's for markets to do. The Achilles' heel of a market economy (outside an economic downturn) is that there is always a labor shortage, always competition for labor—always employers looking for good workers. There is no need for affirmative action. Thomas Sowell in *Markets and Minorities*[26] gives the example of two equally racist brothers. One owns a symphony orchestra, the other a professional basketball team. The brother with the orchestra can afford to discriminate: he can easily find nonminority classical musicians. The brother with the basketball team cannot afford to discriminate: he cannot easily find nonminority players at the required skill level. That brother will keep his racism to himself. He cannot afford the revenue loss from a losing team, from lower ticket sales, from lower revenue from advertisement.

Here is an illustrative graph:

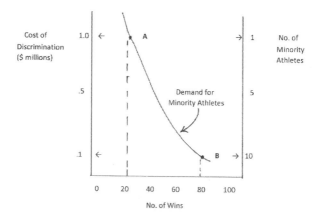

---

[26] Thomas Sowell, *Markets and Minorites* (Basic Books, 1981), p. 26.

At point A, the cost of discrimination is high: with only one minority athlete [arrow at top *right* of graph], with only 20 wins [bottom of graph below point A], lost revenue is $1.0 million [arrow at top left].

At point B, the benefit of no discrimination is high: with ten minority athletes [right arrow], with 80 wins, lost revenue is only $.1 million [left arrow].

Free markets trump discrimination. Money trumps discrimination. Affirmative action, by bringing attention to race, prolongs discrimination.

———————

Why do we look to government? Government cannot solve our problems. Money cannot solve our problems. "If it could there would be no problems."[27] Problems are personal.

Plus, money is one thing this nation has plenty of. In the midst of the Vietnam War, 1964, with an enormous wartime budget deficit, President Johnson declared that it was unconscionable that a nation as wealthy as the U.S. tolerates a poverty rate of 15 percent. "This administration today, here and now, declares unconditional war on poverty in America."[28] Except: 50 years and trillions of dollars of debt later, poverty is still 15 percent, as it was on average throughout those 50 years.[29] Remove those programs now, and overnight, poverty will jump to 22 percent. The increase is what Charles Murray, in *Losing Ground, American Social Policy 1950 to 1980*, calls latent poverty.

Why does government tear down old housing to build new housing? Because it thinks slums breed crime. No, immoral people

---

[27] Overheard in a Black barbershop in Brooklyn, New York.

[28] Lyndon Baines Johnson, "First State of the Union Address," January 8, 1984, American Rhetoric Online Speech Bank, https://www.americanrhetoric.com/speeches/lbj1964stateoftheunion.htm.

[29] U.S. Census Bureau, *Historical Poverty Tables: People and Families—1959-2019*, https://www.census.gov/data/tables/time-series/demo/income-poverty/historical-poverty-people.html.

breed crime. People live in slums because it costs less than living elsewhere, not because they or the nation's economic system are immoral. It's a choice they make to spend their money on *other* things, like professional sports, at $100 a ticket times four for a family of four, iPhones, drugs, entertainment. It's even their choice to delegate responsibility for their lives, fathers, for example, who walk away when their children are born. *That* creates slums.[30]

Housing projects replace older buildings (often better built), but do not replace the people living there—which is why such housing deteriorates, immediately, to be torn down and built again: Western Addition (San Francisco), Cabrini-Green (Chicago), Morningside Heights (New York). Even new luxury condominiums in Visitacion Valley (San Francisco), converted to low-income housing because the neighborhood deteriorated and the units couldn't be sold were immediately trashed, torn down, but not replaced. Replaced was a brand-new public swimming pool for the Bayview District, San Francisco, trashed within weeks of its opening. The mayor, counting on that district's votes, had it rebuilt immediately.

The message: government must not, because it cannot, intervene in a market economy. Regulate business, prevent discrimination—not possible. Humans are a force of nature, water behind a dam that goes around every intervention.

> Deliberately discriminatory laws have been part of the history of the United States, and many other countries. If such laws were always effective, Jews and Chinese would be poverty-stricken around the world, instead of generally prosperous. Even in the *antebellum* South, where severely restrictive laws kept "free persons of color" out of many occupations, the economic advancement of this group continued up to the Civil War, and their descendants continued to prosper and provide a disproportionate

---

[30] Gretchen Livingston, "About One-Third of US Children are Living with an Unmarried Parent," Pew Research Center, April 27, 2018, https://www.pewresearch.org/fact-tank/2018/04/27/about-one-third-of-u-s-children-are-living-with-an-unmarried-parent. The report states that nationwide 13 percent of Asian families, 24 percent of white families, and 58 percent Black families have children with unmarried parents.

amount of twentieth-century black leadership. The problems facing a government seeking to enforce non-discrimination as social policy are very similar to those facing governments seeking social betterment: (1) insufficiency of knowledge of the groups they're helping, (2) monitoring costs, (3) government incentives at variance with the incentives of those seeking that betterment.[31]

Incentives are why Black income as a percent of white income rose significantly after the passage of the Civil Rights Act of 1964, but was that rise the result of the Act or, as Thomas Sowell questions, the result of changed public opinion which made the Act possible also making possible a reduction in hiring discrimination?[32]

———

The conservative position is unpopular:

The U.S. Constitution, a conservative document, protects against tyranny of the majority. A *constitutional* democracy, it prevents 51 percent of a nation from forcing 49 percent to obey laws that are illegal, even if democratically enacted (which did not stop Franklin Roosevelt in 1936, in complete disregard of the Constitution, from threatening to place six additional justices on the Supreme Court and which Congress was considering during president Trump's final days in office [2020] should he have tried to appoint another justice).[33]

Individual liberty, a conservative notion because it implies individual responsibility, does not mean individual empowerment, i.e., individuals with a right to economic and social equality. Individuals have a right to equality before the law, why Frederick

---

[31] Sowell, *Markets and Minorities*, p. 113.

[32] Sowell, p. 115.

[33] During President John Adams' last three months in office, he pressured the Senate to approve his choice for Supreme Court justice, a person incoming president Thomas Jefferson did not want. John Marshall, arguably the finest Supreme Court justice ever, whose *Marbury v. Madison* gave the court the right to disallow congressional legislation it deemed unconstitutional, was that justice.

Douglass and Martin Luther King Jr. both said that all we ask is equality before the law. Douglass, yes. King would not have agreed that citizens have no right to social security, health care, education, employment, leisure, cultural access, standard of living. King advocated for a guaranteed income. What he didn't realize is that taxation, an infringement on the income of others, is mostly paid by the working middle class, not the rich.

Such a demand, a product of the French Revolution's "Rights of Man" and the UN's "Declaration of Human Rights" is without historical precedence. Modern, it allows citizens to claim specific benefits, entitlements without paying for them. But those entitlements are not *general rights*. Citizens today confuse the difference; they see nothing wrong with taxing society at large for benefits that accrue to particular individuals.

The U.S. Constitution protects general rights. Common law protects specific rights. General rights are not to be compromised. For example, the Statute of Frauds, 1677, was a court case between private parties whose decision became law. The statute states that an aural contract to sell land is unenforceable. Get someone drunk in a bar so that they promise to sell you their land, that promise is unenforceable. Since 1677, land transfers in Britain and the U.S. require a signed document witnessed by two people.

————

In the 1930s and '40s, Americans were proud to say they were Communist. Today, they're proud to say they're progressive, willing to move forward with new ideas: the idea of citizens coming together collectively to solve their problems, asking the nation's most intelligent, educated and well-meaning citizens to take the lead. European socialism.

In the 1950s, that exhilaration was expressed by Whittaker Chambers in *Witness*, his account of his experiences as an inner member of the Communist Party, afterward, as a person ostracized for having abandoned the party, more importantly, for also having testified against prominent Americans, Alger Hiss, for one, before

Congress. Today's conservatives, having abandoned their college-day's progressivism for classical liberalism, in a nation 90 percent progressive, feel that same ostracism.

> No one who has, even once, lived close to the making of history can ever again suppose that it is made the way the history books tell it. With rare exceptions, such books are like photographs. They catch a surface image. Often as not, they distort it. The secret force working behind and below the historical surface they seldom catch.
>
> It is certain that, between the years 1930 and 1948, a group of almost unknown men and women, Communists or close fellow travelers, or their dupes, working in the United States Government, or in some singular unofficial relationship to it, or working in the press, affected the future of every American now alive, and in-directly the fate of every man now going into uniform. Their names, with half a dozen exceptions, still mean little or nothing to the mass of Americans. But their activities, if only in promoting the triumph of Communism in China, have decisively changed the history of Asia, of the United States, and therefore, of the world. If mankind is about to suffer one of its decisive transformations, if it is about to close its 2000-year-old experience of Christian civilization, and enter upon another wholly new and diametrically different, then that group may claim a part in history such as it is seldom given any men to play, particularly so few and such obscure men.
>
> —Whitaker Chambers, *Witness*[34]

Instead of "its 2,000-year-old experience of Christian civilization," Chambers might have said, "Its 2,500-year-old experience of Western civilization, as American schools and universities no longer look to their roots, 5th century Athens, 1st century Rome, 18th century Age of Enlightenment, British and American democracy, to warn against today's anti-U.S., woke,

---

[34] Whittaker Chambers, *Witness* (Regnery History, 1952), p. 277.

liberal 'cultural revolution,' as, in the 1940s, they did not warn against the anti-U.S. Communist revolution."

If communism is a tragedy of history, progressivism, a 20th-century phenomenon, is the tragedy of our time. In the 1930s, '40s and '50s, progressives were Communists; from the 1960s forward, socialists.

> One thing I knew: I was no longer a Communist. I had broken involuntarily with Communism at the moment when I first said to myself: "It is just as evil to kill the Tsar and his family and throw their bodies down a mine shaft as it is to starve two million peasants or slave laborers to death. More bodies are involved in one case than the other. But one is just as evil as the other, not more evil, not less evil."[35]

> "How long are you going to keep on killing people?" Lady Astor would ask Stalin brightly. "As long as it is necessary," he answered and asked in turn: "How many people were killed in the First World War? You killed that many people for nothing, and you blame us for killing a handful for the most promising social experiment in history?"[36]

> Stalin's answer was unanswerable. It could only be answered by another question:

> "And man's soul?"[37]

Even if man's soul doesn't exist, morality exists. Outside of self-defense, no one has the right to kill another.

Put people in charge, communism, socialism, you will be in their debt. They will secure their position of power permanently, then, kill you (or throw you in prison).

"Take, and you will toe the line." "From each according to his ability, to each accord to their needs," Marxism, is guaranteed to

---

[35] Chambers, p. 53.

[36] Chambers, p. 54.

[37] Chambers, p. 54.

24

lead to a society where individuals show need rather than ability—then crushed by those in power. The Soviet Union was that society, prison, where no one did more than the absolute minimum: *One Day in the life of Ivan Denisovich*, Aleksandr Solzhenitsyn; *Wer auszahlt ist der Meister, und wer Geld nimmt muss auch etwas geben.* [Who pays is boss, and who takes money must also give something.], Colonel Boris Bykov, Soviet spy.[38]

Governments must not use the means of justice to defeat the ends of justice—lawsuits, regulation of social, political and economic freedom, taxation, police power—to allow the guilty to go free, to allow revolutions to be legal.

"Man is not a means of justice; man is the end of justice." Immanuel Kant. As a means of justice, communism spread its ice cap over Europe and Asia. Populations today are still trying to get out from under that cap, trying to remember how life was before they traded freedom for security (European socialism). It's why, during the Cold War, the U.S. did not come to their defense ("Article X," George Kenan's U.S. foreign policy of containment), why at Yalta we gave Stalin half of Europe, Czechoslovakia, for example, a truly decent country. The reason: Communist infiltration in American government, Alger Hiss, the Rosenbergs, traitors, the reason for the House Un-American Activities Committee: to stop the Communist infiltration. It was that infiltration that persuaded the U.S. not to fight to win in Korea and Vietnam (why General MacArthur was recalled, why the population of South Vietnam was not drafted into the army). *Realpolitik* (à la Henry Kissinger): stop communism from spreading but not actually defeat communism.[39]

No life can be saved which has lost the vital power to save itself. [40]

---

[38] Chambers, p. 354.

[39] Sitting at Senator Joseph McCarthy's right hand throughout the House Un-American Activities Committee hearings was his top assistant, Robert F. Kennedy.

[40] Chambers, p. 679.

In accusing [Alger] Hiss of communism, I had attacked an architect of the U.N., and the partisans of peace fell upon me like combat troops. I had attacked an intellectual and a "liberal." A whole generation felt itself to be on trial—with pretty good reason, too, for its fears probably did not far outrun its guilt.[41]

John Locke

Injury or violence against another person is a trespass against the whole species.

> [E]very man, by the right he hath to preserve mankind in general, may restrain, or, where it is necessary, destroy things noxious to them, and so may bring such evil on any one, who hath transgressed that law, as may make him repent the doing of it, and thereby deter him, and by this example others, from doing like mischief.
> EVERY MAN HATH A RIGHT TO PUNISH THE OFFENDER, AND BE EXECUTIONER OF THE LAW OF NATURE.
>
> —John Locke, *Second Treatise of Government*[42]

In the original, this last sentence is in ten-point capital letters. Why? To make it very clear that natural law is the basis of John Locke's writing, the notion that every man, every woman, has a natural right to their own life, liberty and property, that in a state of nature, one citizen threatening another is a state of war. Because, with no one to turn to for help, such an attack is a form of enslavement with risk of irremediable damage, death, an attack from

---

[41] *Chambers*, p. 697. The Alger Hiss affair was America's Dreyfus affair. Vitriolic hatred of Chambers was the vitriolic hatred of Dreyfus. Dreyfus was sent to Devil's Island, Chambers attempted suicide.

[42] John Locke, *Second Treatise of Government* (Pantianos Classics, first published 1689), Chapter 2, "Of the State of Nature" Section 8, p. 79.

a beast of prey. One has a right, then, to destroy the attacker because there is no way to determine in the moment if the attacker will kill you or not. According to Locke, protection is why man puts himself into society: protection by a neutral third party, government.[43]

But once citizens accept government protection, they also accept they no longer live in a pure state of nature, and they may no longer take the law into their own hands. In civilization, government agents, the police, intervene—followed by legal process where the accused have the right to defend themselves followed, according to Locke, by the offended party having the right to demand punishment.[44]

––––––––

Our Declaration of Independence is verbatim John Locke: the right of citizens physically to overthrow noxious government. At its origin and for 150 years, the U.S. was a Lockean nation. Then, believing the world to be moving forward, 20th-century progressives put an end to that. We are today a Hobbesian nation, a state of overarching rules that leave citizens less responsible for their actions and allow government to do more than protect: provide. Except, nowhere in the Declaration or the Constitution is there a statement that allows government to do this: provide food, clothing, shelter, pension, healthcare, education. Pulled from thin air, these entitlements do not exist in nature. Even the right to one's life, liberty and property does not exist in nature, yet is so essential to our survival as a species we call it a natural right. Civil rights, political and legal equality, in this sense these, too, are natural rights, but social and economic equality are not; they are desires paid for with the labor of others.

---

[43] Locke, Chapter 3, "Of the State of War" Section 21, p. 83.

[44] If "EVERY MAN HATH A RIGHT TO PUNISH THE OFFENDER," perhaps the offended should determine the punishment. Intrude and frighten an unsuspecting person in their home: long and immediate incarceration. Threaten with a weapon: a death sentence— or, let a jury decide. If death, then, immediate. One, because killing a person years later is not to kill the same person, it's murder; two, because only serious immediate punishment deters crime.

[E]very man has a property in his own person: this no body has any right to but himself. The labour of his body, and the work of his hands, we may say, are properly his. Whatsoever then he removes out of the state that nature hath provided [and] mixed his labour with, and joined to it something that is his own, and thereby makes it his property . . . which excludes [it] from the common right of other men: for this labour being the unquestionable property of the labourer, no man but he can have a right to what that is once joined to, least where there is enough, and as good, left in common for others.[45]

In other words, if you plant crops, those watching have no right to enter your field and take what they need. A fence makes that clear.[46] What you produce, no one has a right to take.

He that is nourished by the acorns he picked up under an oak, or the apples he gathered from the trees in the wood, has certainly appropriated them to himself. Nobody can deny but the nourishment is his. I ask then, when did they begin to be his? When he digested? Or when he ate? Or when he boiled? Or when he brought them home? Or when he picked them up? And it is plain, if the first gathering made them not his, nothing else could. That labour put a distinction between them and common [ownership] that added something to them more than nature, the common mother of all, had done; and so they became his private right. And will anyone say he had no right to those acorns or apples, he thus appropriated, because he had not the consent of all mankind to make them his?[47]

Was it a robbery thus to assume to himself what belonged to all in common? . . . Though the water running in the fountain be every one's, yet who can doubt, but that in the

[45] Locke, *Second Treatise*, Chapter 5, "Of Property" [27], p. 85.

[46] In rural communities the expression is, "Fences make for good neighbors."

[47] Locke, *Second Treatise,* [27], p. 86.

pitcher is his only who drew it out?[48] Thus the law of reason makes the deer that Indian's who hath killed it; it is allowed to be his goods, who hath bestowed his labor upon it, though before it was the common right of every one.[49]
As much land as man tills, plants, improves, cultivates, and can use the product of, so much is his property. He by his labor does, as it were, inclose it from the common.[50]

These arguments contributed to the taking of land from American Indians, except that Indians were hunting, not cultivating land. When European settlers arrived by the hundreds of thousands, they saw North America simply as land in nature belonging to no one, to whomever would farm it. Nothing was marked or fenced! Cultural expropriation, yes, except from an economic perspective even if Indians had had clear property rights they still would have lost their land. How it is today is exactly how it was going to be. Settlers had the greater vision. They valued the soil more than did the Indians. They would have paid more for the land than the Indians would have thought it was worth—which is why Mexican rancheros and owners of land in Owens Valley, California, lost their land. In part, by theft, but mostly from purchase by those with the greater vision, investors, for example: William Mulholland, water viaduct engineer, Southern California, who bought land from Owens Valley all the way to Los Angeles; or Donald Trump, in New York City, who purchased apartments at what became Columbus Circle's Trump Tower, by paying more than anyone at the time thought those apartments were worth.

Man being, by nature all free, equal, and independent, no one can be put out of this estate and subjected to the political power of another without his own consent. [Essence of the Declaration of Independence]. The only way whereby any one divests himself of his natural liberty, and puts on the bonds of civil society, is by agreeing with other men to join and unite into a community for their

---

[48] Locke, [28], p. 86.

[49] Locke, [28 ,29, 30], p. 86.

[50] Locke, [32], p. 87.

comfortable, safe, and peaceable living one amongst another, in a secure employment of their properties, and a greater security against any, that are not of it.[51]

Those arguments would have protected American Indians had settlers been forced to honor them, except that cultures without written language, mathematics, knowledge of world history and geography, unless they have a huge army, cannot defend themselves. Coming from such cultures, American Indians and Africans were seen simply as less developed peoples, not as individuals with a property right to their own lives. Unfortunately, neither Indians nor Blacks had enough advocates to speak up for them. Africa, for example, having never even sent an ambassador (not to mention an army) to protest, was too busy fighting British warships trying to stop the slave trade.

> This [creation of community] any number of men may do, because it injures not the freedom of the rest; they are left, as they were, in the liberty of this state of nature. When any number of men have so consented to make one community or government, they are thereby presently incorporated, and make one body politic, wherein the majority have a right to act and conclude [join] the rest.[52]

Communities with a culture of property rights can easily injure communities without one. Unfair to people from an aural culture, but, according to Locke:

> The end of law is not to abolish or restrain, but to preserve and enlarge freedom: for in all the states of created beings capable of laws, where there is no law, there is no freedom: for liberty is, to be free from restraint and violence from others; which cannot be, where there is no law: but freedom is not, as we are told, a liberty for every man to do what he lists: (for who can be free when every other man's humour might domineer over him?) but a liberty to dispose, and order as he lists, his person, actions,

---

[51] Locke, Chapter 8, "Of the Beginning of Political Societies" [95], p. 108.

[52] Locke, [95], p. 108.

possessions, and his whole property, within the allowance of those laws under which he is, and therein not to be subject to the arbitrary will of another, but freely follow his own.[53]

Pure Locke, the above is one of the world's great statements relating freedom to law. It is *the* philosophic basis for constitutional democracy, the affirmation that, in a state of nature, if there is no protection of property there is no protection of life. Couple this perspective to civilizations from ancient Greece to the present with no experience dealing with people living in a state of nature, is it fair to expect European settlers, themselves fleeing centuries of persecution, pillage, rape and warfare, to fully appreciate the tribal cultures they found in North America (or Africa)? Today, four hundred years after they decimated those cultures, Americans do feel regret. When they read Theodora Kroeber's *Ishi, the Last Yahi,* or Zora Hurston's *Barracoon: The Story of the Last "Black Cargo,"* they are truly ashamed.

Our Declaration of Independence is drawn from John Locke's *Second Treatise of Government, Book II—An Essay Concerning the True Original Extent and End of Civil Government.* Chapter 9, "Of the Dissolution of Government," contains the basic statements from which the Declaration is drawn.

> The reason why men enter into society is the preservation of their property, and the end why they choose and authorize a legislature, is, that there may be laws made, and rules set, as guards and fences to the properties of all the members of the society; to limit the power and moderate the dominion of every part and member of society: for since it can never be supposed to be the will of the society, that the legislature should have a power to destroy that which everyone designs to secure, by entering

[53] Locke, [57], pp. 94-95.

into society, and for which the people submitted themselves to legislators of their own making.[54]

Whenever legislators endeavor to take away, and destroy the property of the people, or to reduce them to slavery under arbitrary powers, they put themselves into a state of war with the people, who are thereupon absolved from any farther obedience, and are left to the common refuge, which God hath provided for all men [to fight back].[55]

Sound familiar? If not, you have not studied the Declaration of Independence nor read John Locke. Blame America's schools. For such ignorance, blame progressivism, its notion that we have moved forward from the Age of Enlightenment, the ideas of privileged 18th-century white males, to a brave new world of anti-American multiculturalism, ignorant of the history and culture of British and American democracy.

———

Societies and legislatures did not evolve overnight from man living in a state of nature. Law, custom, language, all evolved over thousands of years—why institutions that have survived hundreds of years like redwood trees should not be torn down.[56] Reformed, yes, provided nature is always the point of reference—because man is always in a state of nature. Think Nietzsche in *Beyond Good and Evil*: There is no need to try to live harmony with nature; you can't live any other way!

---

[54] Locke, [222], p. 149. Note, Karl Marx was correct: social and political relations are determined by the underlying economy. Why, then, did he advocate the abolition of private property? With social and political freedom dependent on economic freedom, private property is the only protection citizens have against government overreach—what allows citizens to say, "No!" to anyone, including government, entering their land without permission.

[55] Locke, [222], p. 149.

[56] To conserve, that is the essence of classical conservatism, the conservatism of Edmund Burke.

Man is an animal in nature. Were Nietzsche alive, he might add, as human behavior evolved over millions of years, so, too, did morality; it's imbued in us, it's in our genes. We need neither religion nor government. From birth we know what to do.

Also encoded is the entrepreneurial desire for personal achievement (at least in the West), a desire to communicate, to produce beyond what we need, beyond even what we think we are capable of—a major theme in the writing of Ayn Rand. If personal achievement is property, government must protect it.

> The great end of men's entering into society, being the enjoyment of their properties in peace and safety, and the great instrument and means of that being the laws established in that society; the first and fundamental positive laws of all commonwealths is the establishing of the legislature power; as the first and fundamental natural law, which is to govern even the legislative itself [checks and balances to prevent any one branch of government from exceeding its powers], is the preservation of the society, and (as far as will consist with the public good) of every person in it.[57]

Meaning, if the legislature has the consent of the people, it will not rule arbitrarily. To Locke, citizens who voluntarily give up personal liberty so that the legislature can function properly will never allow it.

Meaning, the legislature cannot take from any man any part of his property without his consent. To Locke, because the preservation of property is why men enter into society, the very purpose of government, citizens won't allow it.[58]

> The [legislature cannot] do what it will, and dispose of the estates of the subject arbitrarily, or take any part of them at pleasure. This is not much to be feared in governments where the legislature consists . . . in assemblies which are

---

[57] Locke, [134], p. 120.

[58] Locke, Chapter 9 [138], p. 122.

variable [elected], whose members . . . are subjects under the common laws of their country, equally with the rest.[59]

Importantly:

The legislature cannot transfer the power of making laws to any other hands: for it being but a delegated power from the people, they, who have it, cannot pass it over to others.[60]

Otherwise, the nation becomes an administrative state, the U.S. today, with the Environmental Protection Agency (EPA) the perfect example. Congress completely transferred authority to the EPA. Why? Because no member of Congress wants it on record that he or she endorsed or did not endorse a specific environmental law. The risk of non-reelection is too great. But such delegation of power is unconstitutional.

Another way Congress avoids its legislative authority is by deferring to the executive branch. Drawing from Locke's argument that although the legislature is the first authority and represents the will of the people, it needs time to deliberate. No set of laws can handle sudden change: foreign invasion, for example. The executive must administer until Congress is ready. According to Locke, even if the executive always acts in the best interest of the people, still, he or she must remain easy to remove. No dictators.

The *Second Treatise on Civil Government* was written in 1689, one year after England's Glorious Revolution of 1688, their removal of the Stuarts, their "American" Revolution producing constitutional democracy, their installation of a government representative of the people, with a parliament and king constrained by law.

---

[59] Locke, [138], p. 122.

[60] Locke, [141], p. 123.

Constitutional democracy means the majority is constrained by law, that no one is above the law. Again, Locke's contribution to world history is his philosophic basis for constitutional government —that humans in civilization, having left a state of nature, need government protection, but that government must not rule arbitrarily. Drawing on Locke, but also Aristotle, 5th century Athens, and Roman law as promulgated by Tacitus and Cicero, our American president John Adams consistently proclaimed, "We are not a nation of men; we are a nation of laws." Democracy is not unconstrained majority rule.[61]

F. A. Hayek

Here is *the* argument against government provision of services—for which the political economist F. A. Hayek received the Nobel. It is the foundation for this author's writing:

> It is something of a paradox that the state should today advance its claims for the superiority of the exclusive single-track development by authority [government] in a field that illustrates perhaps more clearly than any other how new institutions emerge not from design [not by planning] but by a gradual evolutionary process.
>
> Our modern conception of providing against risks by insurance is not the result of any one's ever having seen the need and devising a rational solution. We are so familiar with the operation of insurance that we are likely to imagine that any intelligent man, after a little reflection, would rapidly discover its principles. In fact, the way in which insurance has evolved is the most telling commentary on the presumption of those who want to

---

[61] The bitter partisan split in America today, as well as historically, is over interpretation of the Constitution. Conservatives believe citizens should accept the U.S. Constitution as a set of rules to live by; progressives believe the majority should not be tied to a set of rules written 250 years ago.

confine future evolution to a single channel enforced by authority.

It has been well said that "no man ever aimed at creating marine insurance as [the model for] social insurance as later created." [Yet], we owe our present techniques to the gradual growth [of insurance]—in which the successive steps due to "the uncounted contributions of anonymous or historical individuals [who] created a work of such perfection that in comparison with the whole all the clever conceptions due to a single creative intelligence must seem very primitive."

Are we really so confident that we have achieved the end of all wisdom, that, in order to reach more quickly certain now visible goals [universal healthcare, for example], we can afford to dispense with the assistance which we received in the past from unplanned development and from our gradual adaptation of old arrangements to new purposes? [Evolution, trial and error]

Significantly enough, in the two main fields which the state threatens to monopolize—the provision for old age and for medical care—we are witnessing the most rapid spontaneous growth of new methods wherever the state has not yet taken complete control, a variety of experiments which are almost certain to produce new answers to current needs, answers which no advance planning can contemplate.[62] Is it really likely, then, that in the long run we shall be better off under state monopoly? *To make the best available knowledge at any given moment the compulsory standard for all future endeavor may well be the most certain way to prevent new knowledge from emerging* [this author's italic].[63]

Written in 1959, this timeless argument reveals why government services are no match for the private sector: government is not creative enterprise. Social Security, Medicare, the nation's

---

[62] A perfect example of market creativity is cosmetic surgery. Not controlled by government, not paid for by insurance or Medicare, it costs a fraction of surgery paid for by government controlled insurance.

[63] Friedrich. A. Hayek, *The Constitution of Liberty* (The University of Chicago Press, 1978) first published 1960, pp. 291-292.

public schools, their natural market forces overwhelmed by government intervention, reduced, now, to borrowing, have lost any ability to adapt.

When government services are failing, politicians never recommend those services be cut back or adapt; they recommend expansion—claiming that "all the experts favor it." Why? Because individuals who become experts in a complex field, doing so because they sincerely believe in what they are doing, will *always* say, "Expand it!" Whereas, to Hayek, "uncommitted economists or lawyers who oppose are not counted as experts. [Why? O]nce the apparatus is established, its future development will be shaped by what those who have chosen to serve it regard as its needs."[64] Public choice theory.

Written six years before Medicare, the following perfectly describes why the price of healthcare in America is three times what it would be: healthcare is provided by the state at a level higher than most people would normally demand, and those who can afford to pay are not being asked to pay.[65]

> We have seen how the practice of providing out of the public purse for those in great want, in combination with that of compelling people to provide against these wants so that they should not become a burden on the rest, have in the end produced almost everywhere a *third and different system* [this author italic], under which people in certain circumstances, such as sickness or old age, are provided for, irrespective of want and irrespective of whether or not they have made provisions for themselves.[66]

The above concealed attempt to convince the public to accept socialized services has led government agencies to also employ public relations and marketing. To Hayek, it is very questionable for

---

[64] Hayek, p. 291.

[65] Medicare provides the best healthcare possible, the most expensive of which is for the last six months of life. On their own, most people would not deplete their savings to pay for that, i.e., leave nothing for their children or grandchildren, but when the American taxpayer pays, who cares?

[66] Hayek, *The Constitution of Liberty,* p. 292.

a democracy to spend public funds on publicity in favor of extending [government] activities.[67]

> Such subsidized propaganda, which is conducted by a single tax-maintained organization, can in no way be compared with competitive advertising [in business]. It confers on the organization a power over minds that is in the same class with the powers of a totalitarian state which has the monopoly of the means of supplying information.[68]

It is voters and politicians receiving their information from the same source: experts protecting *their* interests. Citizens would be better off paying low taxes, 10 percent, then, purchase what they need in the private sector. Government spending on public services would drop by half.

Forcing citizens to purchase health insurance or contribute to an old age pension, because "otherwise, too many people will end up dependent on society," the fear of every progressive, has no basis in freedom. In America, it's unconstitutional.[69] In a market economy, all services are provided by private enterprise. Health insurance, where citizens place health insurance funds in their own Medical Savings Account, about $400 a month for a family of four, would be two-thirds less. Pensions, where citizens invest retirement funds in real estate (with mortgages that pay off and whose value increases over time), blue-chip stocks (with dividends reinvested and whose value increases over time), and long-term government bonds, any one of which would allow contributions to either be half of what they are now, or if contributions are not lowered, to pay double in retirement what is paid out now by Social Security.

---

[67] Hayek, p. 293.

[68] Hayek, p. 293.

[69] From 1933 to 1935 the Supreme Court rejected every attempt by Franklin Roosevelt to legalize his New Deal programs, Social Security, for example, until Roosevelt frightened the court into accepting them by threatening to add six justices who would approve everything and anything he suggested. Checks and balances, out. Constitutional democracy, out. Progressivism, in.

All government intervention in the economy is perverse. If the public understood that government subsidy of agriculture reimburses farmers for *not producing*, simply to keep farm prices up, yet exists because lobbied for by big agriculture (which hardly needs it), the public would demand the subsidy be terminated. Small agriculture does need the subsidy, although for the wrong reason: to preserve a dying industry.

Protecting industries that cannot compete on world standards —in the U.S., steel, auto and textiles (Tesla excepted)—is a waste of taxpayer money, *and*, prolongs the inevitable: the demise of those industries. Less developed nations do this to protect employment; developed nations should not. It prevents natural evolution in the economy, prevents the economy from adapting, protects workers reluctant to change occupations, allows them to stay where they are at the expense of national economic growth. It is fear of unemployment catered to by politicians.[70] For Hayek, it is the reason for tariffs: the pressure of falling prices on transitional occupations.[71] To delay transition is to delay adjustments industries need in order to modernize—such that productivity is higher, workers are fewer, the nation's standard of living, higher.

––––––––––

A great mistake in Western civilization is the continual search for alternative social orders rather than for citizens to improve their understanding or use of the underlying principles of Western civilization. Again, the brilliance and development of that idea, the essence of Hayek's vast work, from *The Constitution of Liberty* to *The Road to Serfdom*, the book that brought down the Soviet Union, plus the essay, "The Use of Knowledge in Society," which argues that things not created by man—language, money—the result of

---

[70] Politicians cater to voters who, unaware that in a dynamic market economy there is *always* a labor shortage (except during a downturn), believe government should do whatever is necessary to guarantee full employment.

[71] Hayek, *The Constitution of Liberty,* pp. 359-360.

spontaneous evolution, cannot consciously be improved by man, why nations cannot consciously plan an economy, that is what earned Hayek the Nobel.

Why, then, aren't the classics of Western civilization, for example, "Pericles' Funeral Oration" (after the Peloponnesian War), not required reading? Why do schools overlook the origins of our civilization? Why aren't schools making students proud to be living in the West, living in social, political and economic freedom? Students should read Alexis de Tocqueville's *Democracy in America*. They should read Pericles' Oration, *the* inspiration for the Founding Fathers' ideal for liberty in America. (See Politics, Chapter 2, "The Funeral Oration of Pericles.")

Hayek continues:

> In the struggle for the moral support of the people of the world, the lack of firm beliefs puts the West at a great disadvantage. The mood of its intellectual leaders has long been characterized by disillusionment with its principles, disparagement of its achievements,[72] and exclusive concern with the creation of "better worlds." This is not a mood in which we can hope to gain followers. If we are to succeed in the great struggle of ideas that is under way, we must first of all know what we believe. We must also become clear in our own minds as to what it is that we want to preserve if we are to prevent ourselves from drifting. No less is an explicit statement of our ideas necessary in our relations with other peoples. Foreign policy today is largely a question of which political philosophy is to triumph over another; and our very survival may depend on our ability to rally a sufficiently strong part of the world behind a common ideal.[73]

Except for America, every nation in the world teaches its common culture as core curricula in its schools. At one time, schools in America did teach the history and culture of British and American democracy, whose roots are 5th century Athens, 1st century Rome,

---

[72] Why today do universities and secondary schools in teaching American history disparage America's achievements and "cancel" those who protest?

[73] Hayek, *The Constitution of Liberty,* p. 2.

18th century Age of Enlightenment, but today, in the grip of postmodernism, the idea that no culture is inherently better than another, American schools do not. A huge mistake!

Not to understand that Western civilization (and its pinnacle political document, the U.S. Constitution) is one of the great achievements in human history—that the rights of the individual precede those of the state—is ignorance. Western civilization is not an alternative among competing systems. Western civilization is an evolutionary step forward for mankind.

If American public schools insist on teaching history from the perspective of non-Western civilizations (which in America means Africa and Latin America), they must, then, extend the school day. Core curricula, the history and culture of British and American democracy, must not be short-changed. According to Hayek in the above citation, our survival may depend upon it.

———————

What is liberty? Liberty is freedom to do as one pleases. Liberty is freedom from coercion by others, freedom to plan and act upon one's personal decisions. Liberty is not collective freedom, giving up an amount of personal freedom for the greater good. Progressivism, identifying with the power of the state, is not freedom. Equivocation over granting power to the state, according to Hayek, is to substitute individual liberty for collective liberty, what allows totalitarian states to suppress liberty in the name of liberty.[74] Cuba.

The progressive philosophy of John Dewey is the basis for American public education. Consider:

> Liberty is power to do specific things. The demand of liberty is the demand of power, the negative side of freedom, and is to be prized only as a means to freedom, which is power.
>
> —John Dewey[75]

[74] Hayek, p. 16.

[75] Hayek, p. 17. John Dewey, "*Experience and Education* (New York, 1938), p. 754.

Mao would have loved this. Societies that confuse liberty with power, security with power, also confuse liberty with wealth, according to Hayek, what allows citizens to appeal to the word "liberty" in support for a demand for redistribution of wealth.[76]

Why would anyone give up personal liberty for the collective good? Because liberty requires responsibility for one's actions, not blaming reality, not blaming racism. Not everyone is willing to make that effort.

Racism makes everything difficult, but it is not the reason minorities are not successful. Racism does not prevent citizens from making their own opportunity. Frederick Douglass said it clearly, in 1864, at the end of the Civil War, at Emancipation: "Don't come around with your social workers to try to help. We know exactly what to do. We've been living in this country for 250 years. We're sick and tired of being told what to do. Don't come around and try to tie rotten apples to the tree."[77]

"We know exactly what to do" meant *get an education*. In 1864, 20 percent of freed African-Americans knew what to do. That percentage hasn't changed [worldwide]. While U.S. Department of Education statistics show that for the last 50 years, only 36 percent of *all* American students are proficient in reading and math. What that really means is, based on their very low test scores today, still, no more than 20 percent of African-Americans are proficient. Their low education, not a legacy of slavery, is a legacy of an aural culture.

Consider Jews. Instead of enslaving Blacks from Africa, what if the American colonies had enslaved Jews from Europe? As they did for the Nazis, Europeans would have rounded them up. Six million. Could slave owners have forbidden Jews to read? Impossible. Even the Pharaoh in Egypt didn't try that. Jews would have hidden books under the floorboards. Culture.

---

[76] Marxists know that you cannot tax the rich; you must *take* from the rich.

[77] Frederick Douglass, his essay, "Self-Made Man," first delivered in 1859, as paraphrased by Robert M.S. McDonald, in "Frederick Douglass: The Self Made Man," *Cato's Letter*, Fall 2011, Cato Institute.

For 2,000 years, Jews in Europe were forbidden to live in the towns where they worked. And were forbidden to own land. At sunset, when the bells tolled, Jews pushed their carts, i.e., their stores, out of town to return to the ghetto. (Read the history of Strasbourg.)

The only reason Jews weren't exterminated earlier is that everyone needed their services. If you were sick, quick, get a Jewish doctor. If you had a legal problem, quick, a Jewish lawyer. In debt, quick, a Jewish banker (and then try not to repay, à la *The Merchant of Venice*). If you needed a speech or a report, quick, a Jewish writer (as Mohamed hired four Hollywood scribes to write the *Koran*, which to Muslims is so beautiful, it could only have been written by God). Blacks, there's your model: be so useful that society comes to you.[78]

———

While we can feel genuine concern for the fate of our familiar neighbors and usually will know how to help when help is needed, we cannot feel in the same way about the thousands or millions of unfortunates whom we know to exist in the world but whose individual circumstances we do not know. However moved we may be by accounts of their misery, we cannot make the abstract knowledge of the numbers of suffering people guide our everyday actions [stop reading the *New York Times*]. If what we do is to be useful and effective, our objectives must be limited, adapted to the capacities of our mind and our compassions. To be constantly reminded of our "social" responsibilities to all the needy or unfortunate in our community, in our country, or in the world, must have the effect of attenuating our feelings until the distinctions between those responsibilities which call for our action and those which do not disappear. In order to be effective, then, responsibility must be so confined as to enable the individual to rely on his own concrete knowledge in

---

[78] Will being useful end racism? No. It didn't end anti-Semitism. In 2015, when a majority of the staff of *Charlie Hebdo* were murdered, President Benjamin Netanyahu of Israel came to France to speak on *national television*. He pleaded: "Jews of France, what are you waiting for? Come to Israel."

deciding on the importance of the different tasks, to apply his own moral principles to circumstances he knows, and to help to mitigate evils voluntarily.[79]

Outside of communism, the only solution to aiding the poor is for individuals, one at a time, to come to the aid of another individual, and continue that aid for 10 years. Forget collective solutions, forget government social programs. Life is too complicated, individuals too diverse. Poverty in the U.S. in 1965 was 15 percent, yet, after 50 years of the War on Poverty, and billions of dollars, now, trillions of dollars (paid for by borrowing), according to the U.S. Census Bureau (cited earlier), on average, to this day, the poverty rate remained unchanged. Remove those War on Poverty programs, now, and latent poverty jumps to 22 percent.[80] Keep those War on Poverty programs and latent poverty may eventually hit 35 percent.

Forget about equality. It is *inequality* that drives a dynamic economy. "Those forces which at first make inequality self-accentuating later tend to diminish it."[81] Reduce inequality by redistributing wealth by redistributing ownership of the means of production. Yes, that will create equality—at the expense of economic growth and standard of living.

The Soviet Union and Cuba got an initial rush of wealth from their confiscation of private property, but from the moment they instituted communism, their economies began dying. Citizens, i.e., producers, turned over production to the state, a nonbusiness entity, then watched those confiscated assets deteriorate. With the economy no longer producing anything, even repairing anything, standard of living dropped. Why didn't the Soviet Union experiment first with one country? Cuba had no excuse. In 1959, after 40 years of Soviet failure, Cubans could have compared East Germany to West Germany, North Korea to South Korea. Eager socialists, they

---

[79] Hayek, *The Constitution of Liberty*, p. 84.

[80] Charles Murray, *Losing Ground: American Social Policy 1950-1980* (Basic Books, 1984), p. 65.

[81] Hayek, p. 48, in the sense that a rising tide lifts all boats.

couldn't wait. Revolutionaries, they knew in their hearts they had the bigger picture: no time to lose, the masses still relishing Randian dreams of personal achievement from producing a product will never vote for communism, owners of private property have to be taught a lesson.[82]

In the West, workers attempt equality through unionization—but their demands for higher wages and benefits almost always exceed market price, and markets adjust. Rather than invest in labor, producers invest in capital, in technology that replaces labor. Communism invests in labor and achieves full employment, but make-work is not work.[83]

The argument for liberty is an argument for principles, not expediency. New ideas should never replace principles developed over centuries, unless tested. *That* idea is the heart of classical conservatism, whose classical argument is that the French and Soviet Revolutions, untested, destroyed rather than reformed their societies.

---

[82] Freedom to a revolutionary is freedom of the wolf to take what it needs, to attack the shepherd's sheep when it's hungry. Abraham Lincoln cited that example when suggesting that America had better agree on a definition of liberty, that freedom to own slaves, freedom of the wolf, is not the freedom he, Lincoln, had in mind.

Not able to convince citizens by putting ideas in their head, Communist wolves, as an expression of liberty, convinced citizens by putting bullets in their head—why Che Guevara, to make a point, rounded up hundreds of homeowners and factory owners who wouldn't turn over their property, lined them up, personally shot them in the head.* Having read Mao, "political power grows out of the barrel of a gun," unlike the German SS whose excuse was "we were just following orders," Che made no excuse for his murders: he was zealously *giving* orders.

*In 1962, the official Cuban newspaper *Revolución* reported that Guevara said, "in times of excessive tension we cannot proceed weakly. At the Sierra Maestra, we executed many people by firing squad without knowing if they were fully guilty. At times, the Revolution cannot stop to conduct much investigation; it has the obligation to triumph." Maxim Lott, "5 Inconvenient Truths about Che Guevara," Fox News, February 18, 2019. https://www.foxnews.com/politics/5-inconvenient-truths-about-che-guevara

[83] For 50 years, producers in France have been replacing labor with capital—precisely why France, a semi-socialist nation, remains in the forefront of efficient industrial production. During periods of economic expansion, unemployment in France ran between 8 and 10 percent (15 percent among those under 25); during periods of economic retraction, unemployment is between 10 and 15 percent (25 percent among those under 25). French café life definitely benefits from French unemployment insurance.

Nations whose citizens are not entrepreneurial yet creative at finding ways of living with less can live under socialism (economic domination by the state), but that is an unprincipled and immoral stance. Cubans, an entrepreneurial people, are able to live on less, but had they not turned to communism, Havana, rather than Miami, would today be the financial center of Latin America.

Without understanding that planned economies fail, that only market economies, a phenomenon of nature, can coordinate production and allocate resources efficiently, Cubans chose socialism. Deprived of an "economic calculus," a term Hayek uses to describe the spontaneously evolved price system, socialist economies have no price signals, no way to calculate relative prices for demand, no way to ration resources such that they naturally go to the highest bidders, by definition, the most efficient users. To Hayek, socialist economies without a price system cannot solve this knowledge problem.[84] With knowledge so vast and dispersed among billions of market participants, themselves each making billions of decisions, only individuals actively engaged in the economy, personally at risk, have the incentive to discover what things really cost, i.e., make an economic calculation. Poorly paid government planners with no skin in the game do not have that incentive—why socialism fails.

Is the free price system enough? Hayek believes that prosperous nations also need social, political and economic freedom. Were he alive today, Hayek would warn China to drop its colonial stance, stop trying to control the world through "foreign aid," investing in and indebting other country's infrastructure—airports, harbors, mines—strategically and covertly establishing bases for future military control. China risks what Hayek calls a "fatal conceit," the arrogance of believing that any nation, let alone a constrained social, political and economic gulag, can do such a thing. The Soviet Union and the Third Reich couldn't.

---

[84] At the fall of the Soviet Union in 1989, Soviet planners were asked how they knew what to produce and how much to charge, to which they responded, "We guessed. We looked at what you in the West were producing and imitated as best we could."

F. A. Hayek, Austrian, was, coincidently, an Austrian economist. "Austrian economics" is the fourth, perhaps last, great achievement in economics. The first was Adam Smith, *The Wealth of Nations*, 1776: that wealth is a function of production, not the accumulation of gold, (which only leads to inflation, why Spain, that stole all the gold from the New World, was then and today the poorest nation in Europe).

The second was J. B. Say's *Traité d'Économie Politique*, 1803: that supply creates its own demand, that anyone who produces something in surplus to his own needs automatically has something to offer in trade, the very definition of supply (and Marx's definition of capital). Every supplier is, then, a demander (the complete rebuttal of which is Keynesianism, which says that demand can come also from government putting money in people's hands—as if producers of real goods and services aren't aware that such consumers are not real demanders, i.e., people who produced something, aren't aware that those demanders will just deposit that money in their savings account in preparation for that Keynesian government policy to fail: the Ricardian Equivalence).

The third was David Ricardo's *Principles of Political Economy and Taxation*, 1817: that nations should produce according to their comparative advantage, that no nation has an absolute advantage over another because *advantage is relative*. Less developed nations always have an advantage over developed nations in producing low-skill products. It costs them less; their cost of labor is five dollars an hour, a developed nation, ten dollars an hour.

The fourth achievement was Carl Menger, *Principles of Economics*, 1871: Austrian economics, that value is subjective, that value is created at the moment, at the margin: marginal utility theory, which solved the 2,000-year-old diamond and water paradox that Aristotle and every philosopher since could not—why a glass of water at home has little value whereas a glass of water to someone dying of thirst in a desert is worth more than a bag of diamonds. ["My kingdom for a horse!"] Because value is subjective.[85]

Economists know these four principles. But that's all they know. Not being businesspeople, not personally at risk, their thumbs not on the pulse of the economy, economists can only predict what might happen long-term. Economists should stick, then, to comparative statics, to providing facts before and after an event that prove their four principles.

In response to *What Should Economists Do?*, a book by Nobel economist James Buchanan, this author wrote a comment essay:

What Do Economists Know?

Nothing—unless we really believe that economists can regulate the invisible hand of nature: markets. Why would citizens of a nation, protective of their individual liberty, want that? Markets are where free exchange takes place, including ideas. As speech is free, so, too, must be the economy, a phenomenon of nature, like speech, that evolved spontaneously, thus, not amenable to regulation. But if they don't interpret and regulate trade, what are economists to do? Human beings are a study for biology, not economics. Even that is questionable, as humans, animals in nature, are born knowing what to do. Behavior, morality, they're encoded in our genes.

Unlike other animals, however, humans produce more than they need. They not only pick fruit, they grow it. When they grow more than they need, the surplus is traded for other things, the accumulation of which is wealth.[86]

Economics is about trade, not production, planning or distribution. Economics is about timing, not about who should have the production; that's nobody's business;

---

[85] Value is not the sum of the labor and materials that went into producing a product. That's "Labor Theory of Value," Marxism. Wrong!

[86] American Indians, philosophers, appreciators of nature, not interested in wealth or property, never produced more than they needed.

those who made it own it.[87] Producers who want more out of life, like money, trade their surplus. Producers, when they have an idea about what to produce, just "produce as much as possible as fast as possible; grab market share before others do; produce more than they need, throw out the rest."[88] The goal: market share. Why? Because consumers, animals in nature governed by habit, remain loyal to brands they first purchased.

There is, however, an Achilles' heel to successful corporations which is, once a founder leaves, the corporation loses market share—why the sole function of subsequent CEOs is to slow the rate at which the firm is losing market share.

Consider Apple. When founders Steve Jobs and Steve Wozniak left, the company crashed. Its stock price fell to near zero. None of the successor CEOs had any idea what the business was about. Jobs had to come back. He did, and the company came back. Against odds, his designated replacement, since 2011, Tim Cook, has kept the company alive. As a professional athlete knows more than meets the eye, so, too, Cook knows more than anyone thought, certainly more than an economist.

The opening paragraph of this chapter cites Hayek's argument against government provision of service. Here is another Hayekian argument:

> Our familiarity with the institutions of law prevents us from seeing how subtle and complex a device the delimitation of individual spheres by abstract rules is. If it had been deliberately designed [law], it would deserve to rank among the greatest of human inventions. But it has,

---

[87] Production is also about increased technology, but that's engineering, not economics.

[88] Remembered from a speech delivered at Haas School of Business, UC Berkeley, in the 1980s, by Alan Greenspan (on National Public Radio). See also Andrew Carnegie's business model: *do not stop production.* Chapter 4, "Gradually I Have Come to Appreciate Andrew Carnegie."

of course, been as little invented by any one mind as language or money or most of the practices and conventions on which social life rests.[89]

Law, according to Hayek, in order that it not be arbitrary, that it apply equally to all citizens, must be general in nature—such that it covers all situations without having to list them. *That* is the beauty, perfection and genius of the U.S. Constitution: it does not account for every issue, gay marriage, for example. The Constitution, by addressing no issues, is, then, relevant forever, why it must be interpreted literally. It was written by geniuses equivalent to Aristotle, Plato, Socrates (5th century Athens), to Cicero, Tacitus (1st century Rome), to Machiavelli, Bacon, Hume, Locke, Smith, Madison (Age of Enlightenment).

Karl Marx does not belong with these enlightened individuals. *Das Kapital*, a guide for dictators, is not classical liberalism. Dense, incomprehensible, it is worse than the UN Charter, worse than the Maastricht Treaty that created the European Union. The U.S. Constitution is one page, the Ten Commandments ten sentences, the EU Constitution 254 pages. Good luck with that one.

Something to consider:

- Law that is general leaves room for creative action by citizens.

- Law that serves concrete ends cannot adjust to change.

- Law that protects individual liberty cannot also protect government privilege.

---

[89] Hayek, *The Constitution of Liberty*, p. 148. Abstraction is the process of reducing from a reality beyond our comprehension some general principles, something we *can* comprehend, the very process of science and philosophy: to make sense of the universe by creating guidelines.

Where citizens are able to adjust to others without worrying every second if they are breaking the law, that, to Hayek, is modern law at its best, preserving individual liberty.[90]

Aristotle said it in *Politics*: "It is more proper that the law should govern than any of the citizens," that persons holding supreme power "should be appointed [elected] only as guardians and servants of the law."[91] Pure John Adams: "We are a nation of laws, not men"—which means: we are not a nation ruled by the majority. We are not a democracy; we are a *constitutional* democracy. The majority cannot just vote for whatever it pleases (calling it "majority rule").

The Founding Fathers didn't make things up. Everything they said had precedent: Solon and Aristotle among the Greeks, Tacitus and Cicero among the Romans, orators who made the public aware that there is no freedom without law—*leges legume* (general rules), that judges and politicians are the mouth of the law, not its creators.

According to Hayek, classical Rome was a period of complete economic freedom—to which Rome owed its prosperity and power. From the second century onward, state socialism advanced rapidly, marking the decline and fall of the Roman empire.[92] With the largest, most technologically advanced army in the world, Rome fell in 476. Roman soldiers watched as the Huns, Visigoths and Vandals sledgehammered the city to smithereens. The soldiers, unpaid, wouldn't lift a finger. Why hadn't they been paid? All tax revenue went to service interest on the national debt.[93] Sound familiar?

The Founding Fathers looked also to the English Glorious Revolution of 1688, which created along with the *Magna Carta,* an English constitution. In 1689 Locke wrote his *Second Treatise on*

---

[90] Hayek, pp. 158-159.

[91] Hayek, p. 165.

[92] Hayek, p. 167.

[93] The Vatican was spared. Attila the Hun, a spiritual person, was persuaded by the Pope, a spiritual person, not to destroy it. (See Verdi's *Attila the Hun.*)

51

Civil Government, the philosophical basis for America's understanding that the purpose of government is to protect life, liberty and property, and that government authority must be limited by strict rules that prevent arbitrariness.

America takes this legacy far too much for granted—the notion that government leaders are elected, that legislatures cannot make arbitrary decisions, *habeas corpus*, due process, separation of powers within government, the Bill of Rights. This history and culture of British and American democracy, almost nonexistent in non-English-speaking nations, should be the core curriculum in American schools. To some extent the culture exists in Europe, but it is not European history. Constitutional democracy exists in Europe today because NATO and the American military after World War II imposed it, as American forces imposed it upon Japan.[94]

Hayek reminds us the Bill of Rights was added as an afterthought. The author of the Constitution, James Madison, thought the articulation superfluous. The argument in its favor was that the Constitution confers so much power on government that individual rights might be infringed if not specifically protected. The argument against, Alexander Hamilton, was that the Constitution was designed to protect a range of individual rights much broader than any document could exhaustively enumerate *and* that the explicit enumeration of some was likely to be interpreted to mean that the rest were not protected.[95]

Hamilton's argument, then, is the best argument for literal interpretation of the Constitution, the best argument against a progressive interpretation which views the Constitution as "rule-of-thumb" maxims written 250 years ago by white misogynist slaveholders, thus, irrelevant today. The political gridlock in America (so far nonviolent) is about *that*: interpretation of the Constitution.

---

[94] Let those two militaristic nations again have an unsupervised military, and the world won't recognize them—why the U.S. has more troops stationed in Germany and Japan, individually, than we do in the entire Middle East.

[95] Hayek, *The Constitution of Liberty*, p. 185.

Progressives won the first battle in the 1930s when President Franklin Roosevelt ordered the Supreme Court to disregard the Constitution and do as he wished: enact all his New Deal social programs. And they did. Roosevelt frightened the court by threatening to pack it with six justices of his choosing, threatening completely to eliminate separation of powers and checks and balances in government. Resorting to wartime powers to create such a dictatorship (considering the enormity of the 1930s economic depression akin to an act of war), Roosevelt and the nation's progressives won that first battle: Fort Sumter.

> For a time judicial decisions appealed freely to the "essential nature of all free governments" and the "fundamental principles of civilization." But gradually, as the ideal of popular sovereignty grew in influence, what the opponents of an explicit enumeration of protected rights had feared happened: it became accepted doctrine that the courts are not at liberty "to declare an act void because in their opinion it is opposed to a *spirit* supposed to pervade the constitution *but not expressed in words*." The meaning of the Ninth Amendment was forgotten and seems to have remained forgotten ever since.[96, 97]

> . . . Fully convinced that he knew best what was needed, Franklin D. Roosevelt conceived it as the function of democracy in times of crisis to give unlimited powers to the man it trusted, even if this meant that it thereby "forged new instruments of power which in some hands would be dangerous."[98]

The following paragraph deserves to be cited in its entirety:

> It is mainly because of the brilliant restatement of the traditional role of the [Supreme] Court in the report of the

---

[96] Amendment IX: The powers not delegated to the United States by the Constitution, nor prohibited by it to the States, are reserved to the states respectively, or to the people.

[97] Hayek, *The Constitution of Liberty*, p. 188.

[98] Quoted by Dorothy Thompson, *Essentials of Democracy*, I (first of three "Town Hall Pamphlets" published under this title [New York, 1938]), p. 21, as cited by Hayek, *The Constitution of Liberty*, p. 190.

Senate Judiciary Committee that this episode [Roosevelt] forms a fitting conclusion to this survey of the American contribution to the ideal of freedom under the law. Only a few of the most characteristic passages from that document can be quoted here. Its statement of the principles starts from the presumption that the preservation of the American constitutional system is "immeasurably more important . . . than the immediate adoption of any legislation however beneficial." It declares "for the continuation and perpetuation of government and rule by law, as distinguished from government and rule by men, and in this we are but re-asserting the principles basic to the Constitution of the United States." And it goes on to state: "If the Court of last resort is to be made to respond to a prevalent sentiment of a current hour, politically imposed, that Court must ultimately become subservient to the pressure of public opinion of the hour, which might at the moment embrace mob passion abhorrent to a more calm, lasting, consideration . . . No finer or more durable philosophy of free government is to be found in all the writings and practices of great statesmen than may be found in the decisions of the Supreme Court when dealing with great problems of free government touching human rights."[99, 100]

The complete endnote to the above citation will follow.

No greater tribute has ever been paid by a legislature to the very Court which limited its powers. And nobody in the United States who remembers this event can doubt that it

---

[99] Hayek, *The Constitution of Liberty*, p. 191.

[100] At the time Roosevelt pushed through his New Deal, popular opinion was on his side: The Great Depression was considered the equivalent to a wartime crisis. Roosevelt needed and the public willingly granted dictatorial powers to protect the nation. Really? Grant the president dictatorial powers because of an economic downturn simply because public opinion was with the president? Do it once and it'll happen again: The Great Society, the Affordable Care Act. The president will declare, and the public will support, every natural or economic disaster as an excuse for dictatorship. So perverse, when one considers that today all economists agree it was not the market but government that caused the Great Depression. Nobel economist Paul Krugman included. Progressive's willingness to jettison the Constitution at any disaster is so un-American.

expressed the feelings of the great majority of the population.[101]

Here is Hayek's complete endnote:

Reorganization of the Federal judiciary: Adverse Report from the [Senate] Committee on the Judiciary Submitted to Accompany S. 1392 [75th Cong., 1st sess., Senate Rept. No. 711, June 7, 1937), pp. 8, 15, and 20. Cf. also p. 19: The courts are not perfect, nor are the judges. The Congress is not perfect, nor are Senators and Representatives. The Executive is not perfect. These branches of government and the office under them are filled by human beings who for the most part strive to live up to the dignity and idealism of a system that was designed to achieve the greatest possible measure of justice and freedom for all the people. We shall destroy the system, when we reduce it to the imperfect standards of the men who operate it. We shall strengthen it and ourselves, we shall make justice and liberty for all men more certain when, by patience and self-restraint, we maintain it on the high plane on which it was conceived.
Inconvenience and even delay in the enactment of legislation is not a heavy price to pay for our system. Constitutional democracy moves forward with certainty rather than with speed. The safety and the permanence of the progressive march of civilization are far more important to us and to those who are to come after us than the enactment now of any particular law. The Constitution of the United States provides ample opportunity for the expression for the popular will to bring about such reforms and changes as the people may deem essential to their present and future welfare. It is the people's charter of the powers granted those who govern them.

Still, it's not enough to have a perfectly drawn legal code. Mexico's Constitution is the U. S. Constitution—but Mexican

---

[101] Hayek, p. 191. In his endnote, Hayek states:
I shall not easily forget how this feeling was expressed by the taxi driver in Philadelphia in whose cab we heard the radio announcement of President Roosevelt's sudden death. I believe he spoke for the great majority of the people when he concluded a deeply felt eulogy of the President with the words: 'But he ought not to have tampered with the Supreme Court, he should never have done *that!*'

governments have not ensured certainty of rule of law. Only deep-rooted democracies uphold the rule of law. Nations without that root usually fail. Singapore, the model for China during the period of Deng Xiaoping, was a middle ground, a democracy within a military dictatorship, but private citizens could still be ordered about, which is unacceptable to Americans.

To Hayek,

> It used to be the boast of free men that, so long as they kept within the bounds of the known law, there was no need to ask anybody's permission or to obey any-body's orders. It is doubtful whether any of us can make this claim today.[102]

And,

> There is probably no single factor which has contributed more to the prosperity of the West than its relative certainty of the law which has prevailed here. [T]he degree of the certainty of the law must be judged by the disputes which do *not* lead to litigation because the outcome is practically certain as soon as the legal position is examined. It is the cases that never come before the courts, not those that do, that are the measure of the certainty of the law.[103]

Ideally, government is constrained in its action, citizens are not. To Ludwig von Mises, Hayek's mentor, bureaucratic government should be given far less discretion than business concerns: "[government] lacks that *test of efficiency* [italics added] which profits provide in commercial affairs."[104] As stated earlier, when government fails, rather than cut back it expands, and we give it more money.

---

[102] Hayek, p. 208.

[103] Hayek, p. 208.

[104] Hayek, p. 213.

Where society does grant government coercive powers, it must [only] be because it advances general and timeless purposes, not specific ends. It must not make distinctions between different people. It must not reflect the difference in political parties momentarily in office.[105]

Hayek admits that the law isn't perfect, that it's made by imperfect humans, nor that it needs to be completely unambiguous. It's why we have judges: to decide if government should act or not. Still, government has no right to control the market, control price, control rent, subsidize industry. Those are particular, not general acts.

It's not government's job to ensure economic equality. It's not government's job to ensure outcome. It's government's job to ensure equality before the law—the only way to ensure equal opportunity.

---

[105] Hayek, p. 226.

2

POLITICS

Politics in America

Twenty-first century America has two governments: Democrats and Republicans. They don't work together. Actually, they revile each other. Witness, for example, how Democrats attacked Supreme Court nominees Clarence Thomas and Brett Kavanaugh: women shrieking in the background during their congressional hearings—the new sound of democracy. Forced to fly to Washington to testify publicly on national television that a young male pushed too hard (without sex). Normally such testimony would have been in the women's home state behind closed doors. That is the new level of political decorum.[1]

How did this split happen?

Because we've drifted away from what should unite us, the U.S. Constitution as intended: government to protect, not provide life, liberty and property—with individuals left to independently lead their lives. Madison's vision was no government at all. Under

---

[1] "We believe you, Anita!" No. Appealing to her duty to woman's liberation, to the NAACP, to progressive hatred of conservatives, Anita Hill was pressured to testify against Clarence Thomas. She lied. Myron Magnet, *Clarence Thomas and the Lost Constitution* (Encounter Books, 2019), pp. 28-32.

pressure he declared, yes, government is necessary in the Hobbesian sense that "not all men are angels"; they do rob, rape and riot. Aware that those non-angels also exist in government, Madison made certain to restrain government with checks and balances: somebody to guard the guard. *Federalist 51.*

We've drifted from what should unite us, British and American history and culture of democracy, because progressives have moved the nation "forward" from a literal interpretation of the Constitution. Progressives want a "living" Constitution, a European Union Maastricht Treaty where every change in society is immediately reflected by a change in law. In the 20th century, progressives have gotten their way.

Progressives have given America a *third* government, the administrative state, where Congress hands responsibility to government agencies. Health care, the environment, public education, immigration—afraid to vote on these issues (where a commitment may cost an election), Congress delegates its authority to government agencies and to the Supreme Court, the nation's new legislature. Americans allow this, but need reminding: "all legislative power in the government is vested in Congress; only Congress can make new laws;" even when the president proposes or vetoes a bill, Congress can still override it.

We take the Constitution for granted. We take for granted what the Founding Fathers created, a minimal state for a self-reliant people. At the onset of the Revolutionary War, Thomas Jefferson proclaimed that if citizens were afraid of democracy, afraid to live without a king, without huge government, afraid to give every man the vote, they could leave. Thousands did. They fled to Canada.

Government exists to prevent citizens from taking the law into their own hands. And that's all that's necessary: a minimal state, a neutral third-party to protect citizens—a democracy where leaders are elected and the legislature makes laws—constrained by a constitution, which means citizens cannot just vote for whatever they want. They cannot just vote 51 to 49, or 90 to 10, to do something illegal. The Enumerated Powers Clause Article 1, Section 8, lists 18 Congressional powers (plus 12 specified elsewhere, thus, 30). Those powers describe what government can do: provide for general not particular welfare, and national defense. Not food, clothing and shelter. That's socialism. Are Americans today so afraid of personal responsibility they cannot see that the nation's success for the last 400 years is due entirely to immigrants from around the world seeking nothing more than individual freedom and opportunity?[2] Escaped from countries where governments were mean and corrupt, immigrants came to America hoping our constitution would forbid government from interfering in their lives. Why can't progressives appreciate what every immigrant knows and wants: no government. It's why Cubans in Florida are Republican. It's why George W. Bush defeated Marge Richards, the well-loved moderate incumbent Democratic candidate for governor of Texas. He got the Latin vote.

THE ENUMERATED POWERS

Article 1, Section 8 of the U.S. Constitution lists 18 original powers with 12 additional in the body of the Constitution:

[Any government action beyond those powers is, then, by definition, unconstitutional.]

- The Congress shall have Power To lay and collect Taxes, Duties, Imposts and Excises, to pay the Debts and provide for the common Defense and general Welfare of the United States; but all Duties, Imposts and Excises shall be uniform throughout the United States;

---

[2] Perversely, slaves from Africa were lured here with the same offer of freedom and opportunity—by their own leaders, another reason why African-Americans have a sense of freedom.

[General welfare does not mean individual welfare, does not mean social security, health care, universal basic income.][3]

- To borrow Money on the credit of the United States;

- To regulate Commerce with foreign Nations, and among the several States, and with the Indian Tribes;

[Why does government prevent the sale of health insurance across state lines? The price of health insurance in New Jersey is three times that in Pennsylvania. That prevention is in complete violation of the "interstate commerce clause."]

- To establish a uniform Rule of Naturalization, and uniform Laws on the subject of Bankruptcies throughout the United States;

- To coin Money, regulate the Value thereof, and of foreign Coin, and fix the Standard of Weights and Measures;

- To provide for the Punishment of counterfeiting the Securities and current Coin of the United States;

- To establish Post Offices and post Roads;

[Why post roads? Why should government deliver a letter for fifty-five cents to the hinterland when it actually costs five dollars, subsidized by those who live in the city who should only be charged ten cents? For economic justice?

---

[3] Madison said repeatedly that the expression "general welfare" should not go in the Preamble to the Constitution, that in the centuries to come that expression would be completely misunderstood. [*The Records of the Federal Convention of 1787*, ed. Max Farrand (Yale University Press, 1911).]

Why should children in the hinterland, whose parents fled crime and culture of the city, receive the same level of schooling as those who remained, when the luxury of living in that uncrowded hinterland is paid for by the property taxes of those who remained? San Francisco sends its property tax revenue to Sacramento, the state capital, which disperses it equally to rural, suburban and urban communities, although urban centers need it much more. For economic justice?]

- To promote the Progress of Science and useful Arts, by securing for limited Times to Authors and Inventors the exclusive Right to their respective Writings and Discoveries;

- To constitute Tribunals inferior to the supreme Court;

- To define and punish Piracies and Felonies committed on the high Seas, and Offences against the Law of Nations;

- To declare War, grant Letters of Marque and Reprisal, and make Rules concerning Captures on Land and Water;

- To raise and support Armies, but no Appropriation of Money to that Use shall be for a longer Term than two Years;

- To provide and maintain a Navy;

- To make Rules for the Government and Regulation of the land and naval Forces;

- To provide for calling forth the Militia to execute the Laws of the Union, suppress Insurrections and repel Invasions;

- To provide for organizing, arming, and disciplining, the Militia, and for governing such Part of them as may be employed in the Service of the United States, reserving to the States respectively, the Appointment of the Officers, and the Authority of training the Militia according to the discipline prescribed by Congress;

- To exercise exclusive Legislation in all Cases whatsoever, over such District (not exceeding ten Miles square) as may, by Cession of particular States, and the Acceptance of Congress, become the Seat of Government of the United States, and to exercise like Authority over all Places purchased by the Consent of the Legislature of the State in which the Same shall be, for the Erection of Forts, Magazines, Arsenals, dock-Yards, and other needful Buildings;—And

- To make all Laws which shall be necessary and proper for carrying into Execution the foregoing Powers, and all other Powers vested by this Constitution in the Government of the United States, or in any Department or Officer thereof.

- No State shall, without the Consent of the Congress, lay any Imposts or Duties on Imports or Exports, except what may be absolutely necessary for executing its inspection Laws: and the net Produce of all Duties and Imposts, laid by any State on Imports or Exports, shall be for the Use of the Treasury of the United States; and all such Laws shall be subject to the Revision and Control of the Congress.

[The Great Depression was caused in large part by the Smoot-Hawley Tariff Act, which levied huge import taxes on all goods entering the U.S. U.S. trading partners retaliated by doing the same.]

- The Congress may determine the Time of choosing the Electors, and the Day on which they shall give their Votes; which Day shall be the same throughout the United States.

- In Case of the Removal of the President from Office, or of his Death, Resignation, or Inability to discharge the Powers and Duties of the said Office, the Same shall devolve on the Vice President, and the Congress may by Law provide for the Case of Removal, Death, Resignation or Inability, both of the President and Vice President, declaring what Officer shall then act as President, and such Officer shall act accordingly, until the Disability be removed, or a President shall be elected.

- The judicial Power of the United States, shall be vested in one supreme Court, and in such inferior Courts as the Congress may from time to time ordain and establish.

- The Trial of all Crimes, except in Cases of Impeachment, shall be by Jury; and such Trial shall be held in the State where the said Crimes shall have been committed; but when not committed within any State, the Trial shall be at such Place or Places as the Congress may by Law have directed.

- The Congress shall have Power to declare the Punishment of Treason, but no Attainder of Treason shall work Corruption of Blood, or Forfeiture except during the Life of the Person attainted.

- Full Faith and Credit shall be given in each State to the public Acts, Records, and judicial Proceedings of every other State. And the Congress may by general Laws prescribe the Manner in which such Acts, Records, and Proceedings shall be proved, and the Effect thereof.

- New States may be admitted by the Congress into this Union.

- The Congress shall have Power to dispose of and make all needful Rules and Regulations respecting the Territory or other Property belonging to the United States; and nothing in this Constitution shall be so construed as to Prejudice any Claims of the United States, or of any particular State.

- The Congress, whenever two thirds of both Houses shall deem it necessary, shall propose Amendments to this Constitution, or, on the Application of the Legislatures of two thirds of the several States, shall call a Convention for proposing Amendments, which, in either Case, shall be valid to all Intents and Purposes, as Part of this Constitution, when ratified by the Legislatures of three fourths of the several States, or by Conventions in three fourths thereof, as the one or the other Mode of Ratification may be proposed by the Congress

- The House of Representatives shall choose their Speaker and other Officers; and shall have the sole Power of Impeachment.

- The Senate shall have the sole Power to try all Impeachments. When sitting for that Purpose, they shall be on Oath or Affirmation. When the President of the United States is tried, the Chief Justice shall preside: And no Person shall be convicted without the Concurrence of two thirds of the Members present.

- The Times, Places and Manner of holding Elections for Senators and Representatives, shall be prescribed in each State by the Legislature thereof; but the Congress may at any time by Law make or alter such Regulations, except as to the Places of choosing Senators.

Politics in America is about a conservative versus progressive interpretation of the Enumerated Powers Clause. Conservatives argue that if a nation can't abide by a simple set of rules, the nation doesn't deserve to exist. Progressives argue that if a nation can't move forward from that simple set of rules created 250 years ago, it doesn't deserve to exist.

> I detest ideologues, Left and Right; I am a pragmatist. It's more important to get something done.
>
> —Barack Obama[4]

> I didn't have any overarching paradigm for politics. My view was you try to get things done.
>
> —James Baker[5]

---

[4] Conversation Barack Obama-John McCain during the 2008 presidential campaign, as recalled by this author.

[5] Peter Baker and Susan Glasser, *The Man Who Ran Washington* (Doubleday, 2020), p. xxi.

The Funeral Oration of Pericles[6]

Our constitution does not copy the laws of neighboring states; we are rather a pattern to others than imitators ourselves. Its administration favours the many instead of the few; this is why it is called a democracy [government for the demos]. If we look to the laws, they afford equal justice to all in their private differences; if no social standing, advancement in public life falls to reputation for capacity, class considerations not being allowed to interfere with merit; nor again does poverty bar the way, if a man is able to serve the state, he is not hindered by the obscurity of his condition. The freedom which we enjoy in our government extends also to our ordinary life. There, far from exercising a jealous surveillance over each other, we do not feel called upon to be angry with our neighbour for doing what he likes, or even to indulge in those injurious looks which cannot fail to be offensive, although they inflict no positive penalty. But all this ease in our private relations does not make us lawless as citizens. Against this fear is our chief safeguard, teaching us to obey the magistrates and the laws, particularly such as regard the protection of the injured, whether they are actually on the statute book, or belong to that code which, although unwritten, yet cannot be broken without acknowledged disgrace.

Further, we provide plenty of means for the mind to refresh itself from business. We celebrate games and sacrifices all the year round, and the elegance of our private establishments forms a daily source of pleasure and helps to banish the spleen [anger]; while the magnitude of our city draws the produce of the world into our harbour, so that to the Athenian the fruits of other countries are as familiar a luxury as those of his own.[7]

---

6 Thucydides, *History of the Peloponnesian War*, Book II— "The Funeral Oration of Pericles, "in *Classics of Greek Literature*, ed. Harry E. Wedeck (Littlefield, Adams & Co.,1964), pp. 260-261.

7 So lucky. A century earlier the Athenians asked Solon, a successful merchant and philosopher, to straighten out their economy. He told incredulous Athenians to produce according to their comparative advantage: olive oil, painted pottery and shipping—and trade for *everything* else. Overnight, Athens became a wealthy modern economy.

If we turn to our military policy, there also we differ from our antagonists. We throw open our city to the world, and never by alien acts exclude foreigners from any opportunity of learning or observing, although the eyes of an enemy may occasionally profit by our liberality; trusting less in system and policy than to the native spirit of our citizens; while in education, where our rivals from their very cradles by a painful discipline seek after manliness, at Athens we live exactly as we please, and yet are just as ready to encounter every legitimate danger. In proof of this it may be noticed that the Lacedaemonians do not invade our country alone, but bring with them all their confederates; while we Athenians advance unsupported into the territory of a neighbour, and fighting upon a foreign soil usually vanquish with ease men who are defending their homes. Our united force was never yet encountered by any enemy, because we have at once to attend to our marine and to dispatch our citizens by land upon a hundred different services; so that, wherever they engage with some such fraction of our strength, a success against a detachment is magnified into a victory over the nation, and a defeat into a reverse suffered at the hands of our entire people. And yet if with habits not of labour but of ease, and courage not of art but of nature, we are still willing to encounter danger, we have the double advantage of escaping the experience of hardships in anticipation and of facing them in the hour of need as fearlessly as those who are never free from them.[8]

A product of the greatest civilization, ever[9], in thought, the Athenian Constitution is *the* basis for the U.S. Constitution—to which was added the greatest of modern political thought, classical liberalism of

---

[8] At the Battle of Marathon, 490 BC, an Athenian contingent fought an enormous Persian army. The Athenians, saving their way of life, literally, Western civilization, fought courageously; the Persians, seeking conquest, had no such incentive.

[9] Fifth century Athens will never be equaled. Its small size allowed for direct democracy— in which every citizen voted on every issue. Influenced by Aristotle, it encouraged intense political interaction. What 5th century Athens achieved in architecture, art, math, science, political science, literature, drama and philosophy is still the basis of those fields.

the Age of Enlightenment: Niccolò Machiavelli, Francis Bacon, Thomas Hobbes, John Locke, David Hume, Adam Smith.

Created by the Founding Fathers, the U.S. Constitution lasted 150 years (50 years longer than the Athenian Constitution), until destroyed in 1933 when Franklin Roosevelt declared a New Deal: the U.S. Constitution, no longer rule of law but rule of thumb, was to no longer be interpreted as are the Ten Commandments and Golden Rule, literally, but as a living document, and mean whatever progressives say it means.

Whoa! A step from a pinnacle in *any* direction is a step down —a step away from minimal government back to aristocracy, why the Founding Fathers are today's radicals (who let citizens make their own decisions), and progressives today's reactionaries (who themselves want to make those decisions).

The Funeral Oration of Pericles has been required reading since its inception—part of what constitutes a classical education—the major writing of the Greeks and Romans whose civilization and thought processes are *identical* to how we today think in the West, only better.

A modern work in a classical education is Ralph Ellison's *Invisible Man*, published by Modern Library, a publisher of America's major classics. The last third of *Invisible Man* describes a race riot in Harlem in the 1940s—identical to every major slave rebellion and race riot in America every 20 years since 1610. Beware, then, of "This Time it's Different!" Four hundred years from now we will still be having this discussion—still wondering at the advice of the Pakistani ambassador to England to his son, a student at Oxford, with respect to racism, "get used to it"—still ignoring the opening epigraph of T.S. Eliot: time past, time present, time future, they're the same.

400 Years

> When you hear about slavery for 400 years, for 400 years?
> That sounds like a choice.
>
> —Kanye West.[10]

Well, why did it last so long? Because there was no one to help. No African king came over and said, "Stop, we'll buy 'em back! And if you don't sell 'em to us, we'll come with a one-million-man army and take 'em back."

Rather, King Gezo of Dahomey, whence came the majority of slaves to North America, declared:

> The slave trade has been the ruling principle of my people. It is the source of their glory and wealth. Their song celebrates their victories and the mother lulls the child to sleep with notes of triumph over an enemy reduced to slavery.
>
> —*The Anglo-American Magazine*, July-December 1854, cited in Wikipedia, "The Atlantic Slave Trade," January 2017

When the former Dahomean kings were asked "Why are you sacrificing thousands of people a year for religious rites when you could be selling them to us?" their response was "Okay, pay us in guns and ammunition."[11]

The U.S. ended slavery in 1863. As with the Egyptians when Moses freed the Jews, so too were 500,000 firstborn sons sacrificed

---

[10] "Kanye West on Slavery: 'For 400 years? That sounds like a choice,'" *The Guardian*, May 2, 2018, https://www.theguardian.com/music/2018/may/01/kanye-west-on-slavery-for-400-years-that-sounds-like-a-choice. West also mentions that, "Once again I am being attacked for presenting new ideas," for example, reminding everyone that Harriet Tubman is thought to have said, 'I freed a thousand slaves; I could have freed a thousand more if only they knew they were slaves.'

[11] Africans were equal partners in the slave trade. From the 9th to the 19th centuries, 1,000 years, half the slaves went east, half went west—a convenient way to get rid of so many people captured in constant tribal warfare, and get paid for it. See Elikia M'bokolo, "The impact of the slave trade on Africa," *Le Monde Diplomatique*, April 2, 1998, as remembered from a section in Wikipedia, "Atlantic Slave Trade," January 2017 (now deleted).

in the Civil War. *Price paid.* So why did American Blacks wait until 1960 to finally demand full freedom? (A touching moment in the Civil Rights Movement occurred at the Woolworth lunch counter in Greensboro, South Carolina, where four brave 18-year-old college freshmen demanded to be served. With raised cane, an older white lady approached the frightened students and declared, "It's about time!")

Blacks made a great mistake associating themselves with the Democratic Party. Why associate with a party that cares for the less fortunate rather than a party that cares about freedom? The less fortunate are not going anywhere; freedom might.[12]

Every sphere they have taken an interest, Black Americans have transformed for the better: music, art, dance, literature, the military, professional sports. Religious and conservative, Black Americans should have joined, then transformed, the Republican Party.[13] In the 1960s, instead of radical liberals, radical conservatives would have put an end to Jim Crow laws.

Identifying with conservatism, African-Americans would gain the nation's respect. Important, because respect is the end of racism.

---

[12] There's always a percent of the population that doesn't care, a percent that's greedy, a percent that's lazy. No economic system will change that. Except to enforce laws that protect life, liberty and property, governments cannot solve social problems. Taxation, wealth redistribution, confiscation of private property, constraints on economic freedom, centralization of public education, social problems cannot be solved through the political process. Social, political and economic freedoms are so inherently interconnected that restricting one of those freedoms restricts the other two—why government must stand back when it comes to the lives of its citizens, and why citizens should heed President Ronald Reagan's advice: "When you hear a knock at the door and someone says: "Hi, we're from the government; we're here to help—run!"

[13] In theory, the Republican Party stands for limited government, maximum freedom, but, in fact, like the Democratic Party, it stands for nothing—why, in 2016, Donald Trump was elected President: because neither party was doing anything to solve the problems *all* Americans care about: the high cost of health insurance, poorly performing public schools, lax law enforcement, illegal immigration. Americans held their noses and voted for Donald Trump. They may again (for the same reason) in 2024.

During slavery, Blacks were deprived of everything, but that doesn't mean they didn't know about life. Among themselves they were dignified—when rebelling, nursing or raising white children, or walking them to school every day. *Everyone* knows how things should be.

Frederick Douglass made his famous "rotten apples" speech in 1864. That speech needs repeating:

> The American people have always been anxious to know what they shall do with us. I have had but one answer from the beginning. Do nothing with us! Your doing with us has already played the mischief with us. . . . If the apples will not remain on the tree of their own strength, if they are worm-eaten at the core, if they are early ripe and disposed to fall, let them fall. I am not for tying or fastening them on the tree in any way, except by nature's plan, and if they will not stay there, let them fall. And if the negro cannot stand on his own legs, let him fall also. All I ask is, give him a chance to stand on his own legs. Let him alone! Your interference is doing him a positive injury. Let him fall if he cannot stand alone. . . . Let him live or die by that. If you will only untie his hands, and give him a chance, I think he will live. He will work as readily for himself as the white man.[14]

Douglas confirmed that earned success is at the center of American exceptionalism. So too, Ronald Reagan: "What's important in life is that you feel what you are doing is important and that you feel you have something to contribute."[15] Douglas and Reagan understood man's natural desire to do meaningful work, to not ask others for help (including employment). For centuries, European aristocracy was satisfied living on unearned income; Americans took pride in making it on their own, making the decent

---

[14] Robert M. S. McDonald, "Frederick Douglass: The Self-Made Man," in *Cato's Letter*, Fall 2011, Cato Institute. [In other words, "We know what to do; we know how things should be; *don't underestimate us*."]

[15] Remembered by this author from an interview President Reagan gave one month before he took office.

and prosperous life they couldn't in the countries from which they came.

Still, the fact that the authors of the U.S. Constitution owned slaves does not mean the U.S. Constitution is a "slaver" document, that the Electoral College is a "slaver" compromise. Frederick Douglass, in the 19th century, and Clarence Page, PBS NewsHour essayist, in the 20th, both unequivocally stated that the Founding Fathers rose to the occasion to create the absolute pinnacle of all political documents.[16] Having just fought the Revolutionary War, then, working so hard at the Constitutional Convention to perfect their document, careful not even to mention slavery (needing the South to ratify the Constitution), the Founding Fathers were in no mood to fight a civil war. Give 'em a break. They knew the Constitution was the ticket out of slavery; they knew they created a beautiful solution to balancing power among large and small states —borrowing from Montesquieu the idea of a bicameral legislature: the House of Representatives, where states send representatives in proportion to their population, and the Senate, where each state sends two representatives no matter what its population—California with 39 million: two senators, Wyoming with 600,000: two senators.

They designed the Electoral College with the same reasoning: give a little extra weight to the smaller states to prevent a tyranny of the majority, whether the large agricultural states over the small urban states, or today, large urban states over the small interior states.

Do we owe African-Americans reparation? We did in 1865. Except, don't the Civil War's 500,000 dead and 500,000 wounded (from a nation whose population in 1800 was only five million) count as reparation? Starting In 1812, doesn't the price the British paid to stop the slave trade count? With enormous resistance from Africa, Britain was forced to impose anti-slavery treaties on

[16] The genius of our slaveholding Founders. . .was in their having the foresight to create documents that had better values than those they practiced. . . . They set up a challenge for the people of this nation to never shirk from the task of making liberty and justice a reality for everybody. A flag that stands for those values is worth pledging allegiance to. — Clarence Page, as quoted in Horowitz, *Black Book of the American Left*, p. 126.

hundreds of remote rulers, blockade distant ports and rivers, board foreign ships at risk of war, bribe chiefs and sultans, spend billions in today's currencies, spend years on monotonous patrols, and die in the thousands from malaria and yellow fever.[17] Africa didn't lift a finger.

That Africans did not come to America by choice is irrelevant. Their one choice might have been to be a slave in Africa and not be treated as badly, but today's descendants of slavery should appreciate the rights they have that they would not have had their ancestors not been sent here: the right to vote in an honest election, the right not to be discriminated against in employment, the right to run for political office, the right to own property, the right to trial by a jury of their peers, the right to a U.S. passport.

> Think about it: we went into slavery pagans; we came out Christians. We went into slavery pieces of property; we came out American citizens. We came into slavery with chains clanking about our wrists; we came out of it with the American ballot in our hands.
>
> When we rid ourselves of prejudice, or racial feeling, and look the facts in the face, we must acknowledge that, notwithstanding the cruelty and moral wrong of slavery, we are in a stronger and more hopeful position, materially, intellectually, morally, and religiously than is true of an equal number of black people in any other portion of the globe.
>
> —Booker T. Washington[18]

> The white people held my people in slavery here in America. They bought us, it is true, and exploited us. But the inescapable fact that stuck in my craw was [that] my people had sold me. . . . My own people had exterminated

[17] David Horowitz, *The Black Book of the American Left, Volume IX: Ruling Ideas* (Second Thoughts Books, 2017), p. 120. Note also: Jefferson as president was so infuriated by the slave trade that he sent ships to North Africa to stop Arab pirates from raiding whole townships at a time to provide slaves for the market.

[18] Horowitz, p. 107.

whole nations and torn families apart for profit before the strangers got their chance at a cut. It was a sobering thought. It impressed upon me the universal nature of greed and glory.

—Zora Neale Hurston[19]

Anthropologist and feminist author Zora Neale Hurston, for 50 years holding opinions similar to Frederick Douglass, was ostracized by gatekeepers of the Harlem Renaissance. From 1943 onward, Hurston was considered unnecessarily heterodox [politically incorrect] in that she opposed the New Deal and *Brown v. Board of Education* on the grounds that government intervention in the lives of Blacks was dangerous and caused dependency. See Katherine Mangu-Ward, "Black Bodies, Radical Politics, and Rebellious Robots," *Reason Magazine* Aug/Sep 2018, pp. 4-5, who mentions also that Alice Walker, in *Ms.* magazine in 1975, revived Ms. Hurston's reputation. Today, Alice Walker, Toni Morrison and Henry Louis Gates, despite their progressivism, acknowledge that Hurston is one of the most important and inspiring Black authors of the 20th century. She was the first to use Black vernacular speech and rituals, and the first to expose how the consciousness of Black women was glaringly absent in Black fiction. Richard Wright and Langston Hughes got the attention (although Hurston did as well between 1937 and 1943), while Hurston ended up in utter poverty working as a maid. She died in a pauper's shelter, buried in an unmarked grave —despite having received two Guggenheims, and authored four novels, a dozen short stories, two musicals, two books on Black mythology, dozens of essays, and a prize-winning autobiography. Still, if Hurston were asked to speak on a college campus today, students would shove a pie in her face for her political and racial incorrectness. Why can't students make the comparison between Ayn Rand's *Atlas Shrugged*, a love story by a Hollywood screenwriter, and Hurston's *Their Eyes Were Watching God*, a love story by an accomplished author? Both Rand and Thurston tell the reader that it

---

[19] Horowitz, p. 122.

is creative individuals in business and industry, no differently than in the arts, who lay the groundwork for society to blossom.

At the end of slavery, a certain percentage of Blacks ran as fast as they could to enroll in school. No question in their mind that was the thing to do. The percentage hasn't changed. Why? Culture. Racism and Jim Crow laws are not the reason SAT scores for Blacks are 300 when college entry requires 500 (out of a possible 800).

SAT measures scholastic aptitude, not scholastic achievement. The test is given so that universities don't waste their time with students who can't compete. Which is *not* the reason for the SAT. The real reason is anti-Semitism. In the 1930s, to stop Jews from obtaining university spots favored for Ivy League Christians, someone had the brilliant idea of replacing knowledge-based entry exams with aptitude-based exams: the SAT. Since aptitude and intelligence are universal, DNA the same in all races and ethnic groups, everyone's test score on the same Bell curve, that made it easy to limit Jews, easy to accept more African-Americans.[20]

The SAT should be eliminated altogether. Performance counts, not aptitude. Those who did well in high school will do well in college. Those who score high in any field do so for the same reason: *they worked harder*.[21]

---

[20] Had African-Americans been high academic achievers, the SAT would have been deployed against them too. The point: colleges discriminate. Today, Harvard uses affirmative action as a vehicle to discriminate against Asians. It turns down Asians with 1600 SAT scores to reserve places for "other" minorities.* Its Z-List and Dean's interest list are used to give preference to students Harvard wants: children of alumni, of the very rich (whose parents donate), descendants of the Mayflower. *Anemona Hartocollis, Amy Harmon and Mitch Smith, "Z-Lists, and Other Secrets of Harvard Admission," *New York Times*, July 30, 2018, https://www.nytimes.com/2018/07/29/us/harvard-admissions-asian-americans.html.

> He had perfect scores—on his SAT, on three SAT subject tests and on nine Advanced Placement exams—and was ranked first in his high school class of 592. An admissions officer who reviewed his application to Harvard called him "the proverbial picket fence," the embodiment of the American dream, saying, "Someone we'll fight over w/ Princeton, I'd guess." But in the end, the student [an Asian] was wait-listed and did not get in.

[21] Do professional sports admit players based on their AAT (Athletic Aptitude Test) or on their skill and knowledge? Barry Bonds was one of baseball's best hitters, ever. (Continued on next page)

Here are some famous members of the Republican Party (1968, not 1868):

- Duke Ellington, James Brown, Sammy Davis Jr., musical geniuses;
- Colin Powell and Condoleezza Rice, Secretaries of State;
- Clarence Thomas, Thomas Sowell and Eldridge Cleaver (all former members or supporters of the Black Panther Party), a Supreme Court judge, a Nobel nominee economist, a '60s radical;
- Alveda King, a niece of, and James Farmer, a top aide to Martin Luther King Jr.;
- Jackie Robinson;
- Alex Haley (who, by toning down the racism in *The Autobiography of Malcolm X,* turned that work into a major historical document).

African-Americans still do not feel welcome in America. When Barack Obama was elected president, Michelle Obama declared, "For the first time in my adult life, I am really proud of my country, because it feels like hope is making a comeback." The issue is real. Black Lives Matter is legitimate protest—not only against recent killings of Black citizens by police officers, but against thousands of killings over the years that have never been reported.[22] Perhaps all professional athletes should kneel during the national anthem.

(Continued from previous page) When asked, "How can you see the ball so well when it comes at that speed?" he replied, "It doesn't seem that fast to me." Some truth; mostly bravado. On the day of a game, Barry Bonds was the first to show, hours before the others. By the time the other players arrived, Bonds had already hit 100 balls.

[22] Tim Arango and Shaila Dewan, "Study's Stark Finding: Over Half of Police Killings Go Unaccounted," *New York Times,* October 1, 2021, https://www.nytimes.com/2021/10/01/todayspaper/quotation-of-the-day-studys-stark-finding-over-half-of-police-killings-go-uncounted.html. The study by researchers at the University of Washington, then published in *The Lancet,* a major British medical journal, revealed that from 1980 to 2018, in America, more than 17,000 police killings were unaccounted for in official statistics. Arango and Dewan mentioned that the British medical community was disturbed: they had always assumed U.S. coroner reports were accurate.

But if the American flag stands for all those who died to make this nation free, 500,000 alone in the Civil War, who died to make African-Americans free (and this nation), then, too, Blacks should stand, reminding themselves how lucky they are to be living here. They're not welcome in Africa where they are considered privileged citizens living in a part of the world to which many are (literally) dying to move. The real problem is that American Blacks are still part of an aural culture, a culture that does not stress reading, math, science and business, making it difficult, therefore, to adjust to life in an advanced industrialized economy. Difficult, for example, to employ yourself when no one else will (although that is how immigrants to the U.S. usually deal with discrimination), difficult to succeed in today's complex world.[23]

Blacks do gain respect (and protection) when they join the police department—although, in 1985, the Black mayor of Philadelphia with a well-integrated police force aerial bombed an entire Black neighborhood, killing 11, including five children, destroying 65 houses and leaving 240 people homeless. No justice ensued. The mayor was not prosecuted. The officers were not punished.

In 2016, in Charlotte, North Carolina, under a Black police chief, a Black police officer shot a Black man. Then, there was a protest, which turned into riots; police cars, city buses and private vehicles were smashed, looted and burned, along with office buildings and the city's convention center. Ten African-American men set upon a white man, robbing, beating and stomping him. A 26-

---

[23] "If we're going to do something about this appalling retrogression on race, we probably need to be radical on both ends [liberal, conservative]." David Brooks, "The Quiet Death of Racial Progress," *New York Times*, July 13, 2018, https://www.nytimes.com/2018/07/12/opinion/racism-progress-income-equality.html.

We? Racism will not die until those persecuted gain society's respect. Society's first impression of an individual must be that he or she is educated, skilled, self-reliant. Brooks' compliment that 87 percent of American Blacks now graduate high school by the age of 25 is not what we're talking about. Educational standards in the nation's public schools today are so low they're meaningless, half of what they were in the 1960s. There is the disturbing fact that 70 percent of Black children are born out of wedlock. (Continued on next page)

79

year-old Black man was shot dead by someone in the crowd. Sixteen police officers received injuries. One rioter was arrested.

Both Philadelphia and Charlotte were spontaneous, thus, understandable reactions, but if respect is the cure for racism, there cannot be a double standard. If the president of the United States is not above the law, neither is anyone else.

Multiculturalism

Since the 1930s, America's problems have been compounded by postmodernism, the liberal notion that since all ideas are a human construct, none perforce are better than others. In the 20th century, communism, capitalism, dictatorship, freedom were all tried. Communism, socialism from the Left, fascism, socialism from the right: 100 million dead.

Since the 1960s, postmodernism transformed to multiculturalism, the idea that all cultures have merit. That the great ideas of 5th century Athens, 1st century Rome, 18th century Age of

---

(Continued from previous page) Very bad, because in free pluralist societies, institutions matter—above all, the institution of marriage and family—because institutions allow the state to stand back, to step in only when individuals can't settle their differences.* Historically, that's how Americans thought about government. The institutions of marriage and family, however, work best when both father and mother are present. With women from Venus, men from Mars, as it were, children need both archetypal forces. In 1965 when Daniel Moynihan wrote *The Negro Family: The Case for National Action*, 24 percent of Black children were born out of wedlock. Today, 29 percent of white children are born out of wedlock, 70 percent of Black children. Dangerous—because when the institution of the family collapses, other institutions collapse. Civilization may collapse. When single-parent families are defended as an element of multiculturalism, when Western nations are denigrated for not focusing on identity politics, emotion and tribalism rise to the surface. Instead of defending the notion that the rights of the individual precede those of the state, identarians defend communal rights, an emotional response, like religion, far more natural than pure reason, in that for 200,000 years such a response allowed mankind to survive. That tribal response will cause the West to decline.
*Goldberg, *Suicide of the West*, p. 262.

Enlightenment are simply one set among many, and that Western civilization, Eurocentrism, is a major cause of the world's problems. To multiculturalists, Western civilization—the notion that the rights of the individual precede those of the state—does not account for communalism, the idea that the community precedes the selfish interests of the individual, that the purpose of government is to ensure social and economic equality. This is why to the French, the essence of civilization is mankind controlling nature, controlling markets, not the other way around.

Thus, in the U.S., multiculturalists believe the Constitution should not be taken literally. Society has "progressed" beyond the classical liberalism of the Founding Fathers. So much so, that it has actually achieved progressivism's goal: European socialism—the idea that there is more to life than individual liberty, the idea that society also needs strong central government to secure social and economic equality. *That* is the vision behind Presidents Woodrow Wilson and Franklin D. Roosevelt and Plato's *Republic*: highly trained nonpartisan elites planning and administering the nation. Progressivism. Aristocracy.

———————

Why are progressives so interested in non-Western cultures, cultures that elevate the community above the individual? Because all cultures have something to offer? Because 5th century AD Mayans, for example, gave us the number zero, which they developed to express the number of people remaining in a neighboring village after it was raided for human sacrifice?

Progressives, you're trampling on the most fragile of all notions: individual liberty. You're trampling on Aristotle—who thought like us, only better. Catholicism is based on his reasoning. Just as our blue planet is a miracle, 5th century Athens—in art, architecture, philosophy, politics, ethics, literature, mathematics and science—was a miracle. Read the Greek and Roman masters. Stop reading modern works until you have a basis for comparison. University students, stop focusing on current issues. Focus on

Athens and Rome before you focus on issues with which you identify. Focus on U.S.-British history and culture of democracy— the platform upon which you stand that makes you so confident to advocate for its demolition. Appreciate America's core values, not America's failings. As if no other country or culture would have done those things, as if had you been in power you would not have done those things.[24] According to historian Johan Goldberg, we must not let America lose a coherent image of itself and become a nation that no longer knows what it lives for.[25]

Yes, there is something to learn from every culture—if time permits. "If time permits" means schools must lengthen their day, or year, or add a year to graduation. Otherwise, multicultural education replaces core curriculum and students are deprived of a basic education. To replace the thought process that led to American democracy, to the world's greatest political document, the U.S. Constitution, with details of life under slavery, serves no purpose. Students come home from school depressed and hating America. No country in the world teaches children to hate themselves and their country. Bravo. Drawing attention to racism will not eliminate it. Blowing air on a fire fuels it. According to Thomas Sowell, "Our children and grandchildren may yet curse the day we began hyping race and ethnicity. There are countries where that has led to slaughters in the streets but you cannot name a country where it has led to greater harmony."[26] To denigrate the Constitution because its

---

[24] When asked, "Why is it when one looks closely at the people in history one most admires, one finds at least one thing completely and unacceptably incongruous?" Aristotle responded, "They're human; they dropped the ball." Thomas Jefferson, in his youth, declared that African slaves and American Indians are absolutely no different than anyone else, that America was going to pay a big price for what it was doing to them. *Notes on the State of Virginia.* Older, with respect to Blacks, Jefferson forgot about that.

Not about the Indians—the reason the Lewis and Clark Expedition was a success: Jefferson placed women on the boats so that Indians in unknown tribal lands would understand the expedition was not a war party. Brilliant.

[25] Nick Gillespie, "The Tribe of Liberty," interview of Jonah Goldberg, *Reason Magazine,* October 2018), p. 52.

[26] Thomas Sowell (@ThomasSowell), Nobel-nominated economist, "Our children," *Twitter,* March 23, 2021, https://twitter.com/thomassowell/status/1374346872891047941?lang=en

authors were slaveholders is to commit a cardinal error in philosophy: equating correlation with causation, racism with slavery, racism with capitalism. Huge error. Slavery was as much a part of African culture as it was of Greek and Roman culture. Racism in America evolved at the end of slavery as the result of a people from a lesser-developed civilization suddenly demanding full equality. 1864. Students must learn that although the Constitution protects social, political and economic freedom, it does not guarantee social or economic equality. It guarantees equality before the law, why both Frederick Douglass and Martin Luther King Jr. had the good sense to limit their demand to *that*, to the foundation of this nation, equality before the law.

That's what schools should teach—that America is not a socialist economy, that such things as universal basic income (for which later King did advocate), welfare (which includes more whites than Blacks), and redistribution of the wealth are not what this nation is about. America is about individual responsibility, freedom and opportunity. Beware of forced social and economic equality; they are traps that fuel racism. Provide workers with everything they need in exchange for their political rights—Bismarck, Mussolini, Hitler, National Socialism—and society will return from where it emerged, communal—to what Johan Goldberg, in *Suicide of the West*, calls a return to the tribal instinct hard-wired in our genetic code, the survival instinct that brought us through our first 200 to 300 thousand years, a return to group loyalty.[27] To Goldberg, the problem with freedom is that it does not replace the need for tribal life. It does not replace society's romantic desire, à la Jean-Jacques Rousseau, for a return to nature, for elimination of private property, for Utopia, for refuge in childhood irresponsibility.

Western students, you cannot go back. You would be miserable experiencing the trauma of a communal society operating in an advanced industrialized world. The Soviet Union, Cuba and

---

[27] Jonah Goldberg, *Suicide of the West: How the Rebirth of Tribalism, Populism, Nationalism, and Identity Politics is Destroying American Democracy* (Crown Publishing Group, 2018), p. 30.

North Korea survive because they are totalitarian, the only way to prevent citizens from leaving.

Will China prove the exception? Will "Render unto the West those things that are the West's, unto China those things that are China's" allow China to survive as a totalitarian state? Perhaps. With no history of individual freedom, the Chinese seem willing to render ownership of the means of production to the state, provided, as individuals, they keep some ("communism with Chinese characteristics"), and provided they keep some of their culture. The Chinese will accept totalitarianism if they can hold on to their two desires: to make money and to be with their family. Still, to make certain, China's government further diverts citizens' attention away from democracy by fueling China's ancient megalomaniacal fantasy of conquering the "uncivilized" world. Contrast that to what Americans learn (or used to), what Alexis de Tocqueville warned citizens to prevent: power centralized in the hands of the state; citizens reduced to atoms; collective willingness to sacrifice liberty for a comfortable life.[28]

Through its schools, the West must constantly remind itself just how fragile democracy is, that it must never be taken for granted. Thomas Jefferson initiated public schools for one reason: to ensure that citizens would recognize threats to democracy. From populist would-be dictators, from entropy, the natural tendency of all things to disintegrate—for example, humanity's natural tendency to revert to tribalism, religion, nature, and to believing that man once lived in peace and harmony in a golden age until he was enslaved by the laws of private property and economic freedom (Rousseau). Nonsense. To Francis Fukuyama, as violence is rooted in human behavior (Cain and Abel), government's first duty is to protect citizens from that violence. If a similar proportion of people died from violence in the 20th century as died in most prehistoric societies, the death count of the 20th century—arguably mankind's bloodiest—would not be 100 million (from fascist and communist socialism), but two billion, 20 times greater—because in small-scale

---

[28] "Alex de Tocqueville, The French Exception," *The Economist*, August 11, 2018, p. 55.

tribal societies, one-third of humans died from raids. Casualties were high because prisoners were not taken. The goal: exterminate the opponent.[29] Sound familiar?

How did the shift from Western civilization to multiculturalism come about? The West rediscovered the East: a reverse renaissance. Weary of individual responsibility and longing for a return to communal thought and action, Latin America, the Middle East and Africa look attractive.

Or is it because citizens in the West take Western civilization for granted? That would explain why U.S. citizens undervalue their Constitution, why they have no hesitation to add concepts to it that don't belong.

The shift came about because multiculturalists value individual security more than they value individual freedom—why they abandon principles of individual liberty to achieve (in their minds) a greater collective good: economic and social equality, as if beyond political equality, social and economic equality are possible, as if the U.S. Constitution wasn't designed to prevent such an attempt. Outside socialist totalitarianism, social and economic equality are not possible. People are very different. They have different goals. They are not willing to make the same sacrifices— why F. A. Hayek understood that social justice is a mirage, that there is no entity called society to redistribute wealth or recalibrate social order, only individuals who belong to political factions who vie for power and then wield it through power of the state. The following would be a perfect epithet for the 20th century: "A socialist experiment for which 100 million gave their lives."

---

[29] Goldberg, *Suicide of the West*, p. 30, where Goldberg cites Steven Pinker, "A History of Violence," *New Republic*, March 18, 2007, https://newrepublic.com/article/77728/history-violence.

How prevalent is postmodern multiculturalism? Go to the theater. Cohorts of today's "theater of concurrence" assume that everyone, including their audiences, shares their political views—why today's political plays are written with no attempt to persuade dissenters to change their minds: the audience is taken for granted. That explains why the Left was so disoriented by the election of Donald Trump: they took for granted that he had no electability.[30]

Not always the case. In the 1960s, Students for a Democratic Society (SDS) declared, "We are people of this generation who will be taking action because the Democratic and Republican parties are not leading the way." Fifty years later, with the Left completely ignoring the Right, the Right grabbed that declaration—and used it to put Donald Trump into office.

Today's Left is not ideological. It is a social construct based on the values of the moment. One such value is "Don't take the Constitution literally!" Why? Because with fixed rules, the Left cannot impose its beliefs on others, acquire power, convince others of its moral superiority.[31] In 1937, Franklin Roosevelt's threat to add six justices to the Supreme Court, a real threat to checks and balances in government, was akin to simultaneous power grabs by Hitler and Stalin—and for the same reason: national socialism. In 1959, it was Che Guevara, who personally lined up hundreds of

---

[30] Terry Teachout, "The Theater of Trump," in *Commentary*, November 2017.

[31] The San Francisco Board of Supervisors fired the interim mayor London Breed (2018), a Black woman who had worked her way up from poverty, exactly the kind of person San Francisco liberals claim to support, because the board later realized she was a *moderate* (thus not representative of San Francisco, which is far-Left). They replaced her with a Silicon Valley venture capitalist, thinking he would be easier to defeat in the upcoming election.

> Some analysts see Ms. Breed's removal as a cold political calculus by the city's progressive faction: removing her from office would give them a better shot at reclaiming the mayor's office.

> Peter Ragone, a Democratic political consultant for former mayor, now Governor Gavin Newsom, said, "What I've learned over the years in San Francisco is that for progressives it is not about conscience or ideology, it's about power."

--Thomas Fuller and Conor Dougherty, "Clash of Technology, Race and Politics in San Francisco City Hall," *New York Times*, January 24, 2018, https://www.nytimes.com/2018/01/24/us/san-francisco-mayor-breed-farrell.html.

"bourgeois" property and factory owners (who resisted turning over their property to the state), put a gun to their heads and pulled the trigger. His reasoning: something like, "You just don't understand the beautiful future we have envisioned for you. We know in our hearts that we are doing the right thing. You will thank us later."

Blinded by such thinking, the Left today could never write a play such as *Major Barbara*, in which George Bernard Shaw, a socialist, went out of his way to present both sides. So successful was Shaw that those on the Right have to be reminded the play is not about them.

Go to an art gallery. Identarian artists have usurped the art world. They have turned art that grapples with inner life and beauty into art that reflects identities—radical feminists, the racially aggrieved, left-wing politicos, anti-capitalists, gender theorists.

Identarians have turned art into collective rather than individual enterprise. Postmodernism is about power, not truth, about who gets to express what, who gets to evaluate it. To identarians, the party most marginalized has the moral claim to dictate how its oppression will be expressed, although within that world, rules are completely conformist. Disagree, and your work won't be shown or discussed in an art journal; you'll not be offered a university position.[32]

---

[32] At the Sorbonne, one of France's great universities, activists prevented the staging of a play by Aeschylus: to protest the wearing of masks and dark makeup by white actors. A creative production was halted after hours of preparation because some students wanted to make a point. A salient example of cancel culture.

French politicians, high-profile intellectuals, journalists, Left and Right, have been warning France not to get swept up by progressive American ideas on race, gender and ethnic post-colonialism—because they are undermining French democracy that goes out of its way *not* to mention race, gender, or ethnicity in public affairs. According to France's Education Minister, Jean-Michel Blanquer, "There's a battle to wage against an intellectual matrix from American universities—which are complicit also in providing intellectual support to Islamic terrorism (as the woke Left consider Islam a religion of the underprivileged)." Norimitsu Onishi, "In Simmering Race and Gender Struggle, France Blames U.S. Ideas," *New York Times*, February 10, 2021, https://www.nytimes.com/2021/02/09/world/europe/france-threat-american-universities.html

Identarian art finds justification in the work of a new class of hyper-ideological critics, much as the old Soviet hatchet men upheld Socialist realism. Today it is a new generation of journalists, academics and social-media personalities who defend the primacy of group identity in art. Say what you will about the Soviet critics, at least they were erudite. Not so with today's identarian critics, who care little for art history and aesthetics. What they are blessed with is lots of opinions about everything—all of which invariably revolve around race, gender, class power and privilege. Call them the New Philistines.[33]

Why I Can't Read *Guns, Germs, and Steel*

For the last 13,000 years, since the end of the last Ice Age, three societies developed: literate industrial societies with metal tools, nonliterate farming societies, and hunter-gatherer societies with stone tools. The literate societies conquered or exterminated the other two. This, according to Jared Diamond, author of *Guns, Germs and Steel*, is the most basic fact of world history. The reason, however, according to Diamond, remains uncertain and controversial.

Stop! The reason is crystal clear—survival of the fittest. The conquering societies did what the others should have done: one, stopped moving around—which is necessary for thinking, because when you're moving around, you can't and shouldn't think, you need to watch where you're going; two, they started writing—which is necessary to develop and test ideas, because you can't develop abstract ideas, especially in science and mathematics unless you write them down; and three, started trading—which is necessary for progress because trading societies learn from each other—in that societies can't progress if they're dependent solely upon their own ideas.

---

[33] Sohrab Ahmari, *The New Philistines* (Biteback Publishing 2016), p. 24.

Diamond's notion that the arbitrary layout of continental geography is the explanation for the differing rates at which civilizations developed may be true, but it's meaningless. With trade, ideas travel. With time, civilizations catch up with each other (*if they want to*).

What sped technological development in the West was Western civilization itself: its focus on the individual, not the community. *That* unleashed the urge to produce, a creative and individual act. What 5th century Athens, a city of fewer than 200,000 accomplished in philosophy, poetry, history, drama, politics, art, architecture, science and math, could not have occurred otherwise.[34] Then, because Greece was a trading society, their ideas spread throughout the region.

The notion that civilization should focus on the individual, because that unleashes the creative desire to produce, is true provided individuals are allowed to *keep* what they produce—their art, their crops, their manufactures, the land they personally cultivate. If individuals are not secure in their life, liberty and property, secure in the pursuit of their personal interests, production will not occur. This by-product of Western civilization, the incentive to produce, explains Western success (and *is* the answer to Yali's question).[35]

That's not the whole explanation. Any civilization that unleashes the desire to create wealth will solve life's basic material problems—food, clothing, shelter, health care, education, employment, safety, even environmental protection. But Western civilization goes further; it also solves mankind's need for social,

---

[34] For a nation's schools not to place the study of 5th century Athens, the greatest civilization *ever*, and its follow-up, 1st century Rome, then 18th century Age of Enlightenment, at the center of all study, as core curriculum, is to return Sisyphus and his stone to the bottom of the hill.

[35] During the Renaissance, the rebirth of Western civilization after 1,000 years of darkness, individuals began signing their name to what they produced (a thoroughly Western concept), which proved to be an incentive. With personal recognition (swelling of the ego), individuals were inspired to outdo each other. In furthering production, the importance of competition must not be underestimated (which is the answer to Yali's question, "Why do first world nations have so much material wealth while his New Guinea island culture, by comparison, has nothing?").

political and economic freedom. Psychological freedom, which comes from living in a communal society where life's basic material, even spiritual and aesthetic needs, are solved for you, also appeals to citizens in the West, but that is because those citizens do not fully understand the importance of economic freedom and the extent to which economic freedom underpins a high standard of living, and, underpins social and political freedom. Citizens in the West today take too much for granted. Follow romanticized leaders such as Che Guevara—whose Communist philosophy was so antithetical to Western civilization that the only way to inaugurate it was to force citizens to conform to a centrally planned economy (for the sake of communism, for the sake of The Revolution, for the sake of the nation). Force middle class property and factory owners to turn over their property or receive a bullet to the head (which Che delivered personally, to hundreds). Yet, force citizens to give up economic freedom, the opportunity to engage in a dynamic economy, and your nation marches straight back to serfdom. Cuba.

Why do socialist governments need to control the lives of every citizen? Because, should they grant freedom to even one citizen, everyone else will ask for it.[36] The Catholic Church knows this well. For 2,000 years, its operating principle has been to prevent independent thought and action. Like Islam, the church claims the absolute and fundamental necessity of strict adherence to God's law. Like Islam, the church protects its political and economic power, which it would lose should followers start thinking for themselves— one reason the church prevented Galileo from declaring that not everything in the universe revolves around Earth (and put him under house arrest for life), why it excommunicated Martin Luther, why it expelled all Jews from Spain. Their ideas were a threat.[37]

Socialist governments are identical. Their underlying religion, socialism, crumbles once followers are allowed to think for

---

[36] In communist countries, Cuba, the former Soviet Union, no one is allowed to leave. Leaving exposes to those remaining and to the outside world that the system is a failure.

[37] The church is not completely wrong. As in psychoanalysis, in that no individual can analyze himself or see himself as others do, so, too, according to Catholicism, no individual can achieve spiritual union with God without intermediation of a priest.

themselves. Thus, Western civilization, whose very definition is independent thought and action, is not just an alternative among many; it is an evolutionary step forward.

Diamond doesn't understand this. Nor does he understand that prosperity is a function of production, not geography, and the exchange of goods, services and ideas.

Diamond doesn't understand that if society doesn't produce, it won't trade, and if it doesn't trade, it will have no idea what other societies are doing—that those other societies may be on course to extinguish them. In Africa, thousands of languages are spoken. Rather than a sign of cultural sophistication, it is a sign that people aren't talking to each other, aren't trading with each other. Cultural sophistication is an entire continent speaking one language, the language of the culture that dominates trade and commerce.

In studying the evolution of human society, Diamond believes it is not enough to simply go back 3,000 years to the development of writing, because 99.9 percent of the history of the human species existed before that. Yes, but so too did 99.9 percent of all species exist before that, and they all died out. What's important is to study those species which survived. This may even be the primary focus of *Guns, Germs and Steel,* but removed from the context of Western civilization, the author's notions of geography and literate society summarized in the book's preface and the prologue, *Yali's Question,* are so profoundly wrong that readers are forced to respond by supplying three paragraphs of their own for every one written by the author, which, of course, kills the desire to read any further.

Free Speech

Freedom of speech does not mean freedom to offend. A far cry from the First Amendment, yet today, this flawed theory is what the Left believes.

Let a nation focus on discrimination and equality, on empowering the aggrieved, and tolerance will no longer be the ability to tolerate things we don't like, but the ability to keep quiet, to refrain from saying what *others* dislike: today's tyranny of the majority.

Today's majority culture of identity politics and cultivation of the victim (the grievance lobby, according to Danish author Flemming Rose), has succeeded in shifting the fulcrum of the human rights debate from free speech (what the ACLU still defends, although less adamantly) to the necessity of countering hate speech. In other words, a shift from the individual pursuing individual liberty to the individual aggrieved by the liberties taken by others.[38]

Let free speech no longer mean freedom to offend, let those aggrieved by free speech be cosseted while those whose speech is offensive are assaulted—in the case of college lecturers, verbally and physically, and in the case of those who speak against Islam, with death—and democracy is compromised.

Consider Stéphanie Charbonnier, editor of the satiric French weekly, *Charlie Hebdo*, who declared, before the massacre of her staff, that *Charlie Hebdo* had no option but to continue scorning, mocking and ridiculing Islam until doing so became as banal and uncontroversial as it was in the case of Catholicism. According to Rose, behind those words lay the idea that one of the functions of religious satire is to keep religious doctrine and institutions in check, ensuring they not become sacrosanct and inviolable, not exploited to gain power or social control. Rather, religious satire demands that religious institutions be removed from their pedestal whenever they make claims that challenge the secular order of individual liberty.[39]

Consider United Nations Article 20, paragraph 2, adopted in 1953 as part of an International Covenant on Civil and Political

---

[38] Flemming Rose, *The Tyranny of Silence (How One Cartoon Ignited a Global Debate on the Future of Free Speech)* (Cato Institute, 2014), p. 152.

[39] Rose, p. 282.

Note: Political power is always held indirectly. Pre-science, it came via priests, who represented the mysterious, the unknown, the afterlife, who spoke on behalf of the leader, who told the population to obey that leader or face eternal damnation.

Rights. The majority of Western democracies voted against it, citing its vagueness and the accompanying risk of abuse—that it would be used to silence critical voices. Eleanor Roosevelt, who presided over work on the Universal Declaration of Human Rights, warned against the wording's lack of distinction between words and actions. Who, then, supports Article 20, Paragraph 2? The Organization of the Islamic Conference (OIC), Russia, China and countries that wish to safeguard themselves from criticism on human rights.[40]

In France, the staff of *Charlie Hebdo* was massacred for insulting Islam, for printing cartoons similar to those published by the Danish journal *Jyllands-Posten*—Muhammad with a bomb in his turban—but most of what *Hebdo* satirized was France's past colonialism and treatment of Arabs and Islam. Most of *Hebdo*'s criticism was directed against the Far Right, politicians such as Jean-Marie Le Pen, and their stance on anti-immigration. The attack, however, marked the end of that idealism. It marked the end of the idealism of May 1968. The rebels of the Parisian barricades of the 1960s and '70s were murdered by the sons of those they sought to defend—although Iran, as it put out a death warrant for Flemming Rose (author of the above citations), held a competition for cartoons that satirized the Holocaust, to say that it didn't happen![41]

We're in the 21st century now. Persecuted minorities are quite capable of defending themselves, certainly in the West. With few exceptions, people today are not forced to do things against their will. To believe they are is to reverse the notion of tolerance, to allow those who feel persecuted, the voluntary listener of free speech, to accuse a speaker of strongly opinionated speech to be branded as intolerant or racist. This new intolerance, found especially on college campuses, is not being called by its proper name: fascism.

----

[40] Rose, p. 245.

[41] Rose, pp. 286-287.

Censorship equates words with deeds; it silences words, imposes the norms of one group on all other groups, the very reason public debate in the U.S. does not exclude speech and opinions that are hateful or offensive. To do so undermines the equality of citizens in public discussion; it sows doubt as to the legitimacy of government.

> Here is where the link between tolerance, liberty and equality in a multicultural society becomes clear. To ensure equality, public debate must allow all utterances of opinion, regardless of their nature; and in a society such as the United States, which was founded on immigration, the government [including universities] must remain neutral when it comes to the nature of its citizens' speech.[42]

> The freedoms that allow bigots to bait minorities are also the very freedoms that allow Muslims and Jews to practice their faiths freely. By further eroding those freedoms, no one is more than a political majority away from being the target rather than the beneficiary of laws against hatred and offense.[43]

In a multicultural world where individual rights are replaced by the right to be respected, free speech is punishable. Satire is punishable. It means if one group is protected, others are deprived of their right to voice their opinions about that group.

This means that on college campuses—one of the West's paramount arenas of confrontation with and consideration of *all* ideas—if young people can claim the right not to be offended or claim that campuses should be safe spaces from ideological and

---

[42] Rose, p. 294. That quote belongs in the *Federalist Papers*. However, a quote that doesn't belong is UC's warning to its professors to "watch your language," to refrain from saying "America is a melting pot." Why? Because it sends the signal that the speaker expects minorities to assimilate to the dominant culture.*

What UC is really doing, rather than protecting free speech, is protecting free silence, the right of citizens (students) not to hear ideas they don't like. (And why shouldn't minorities, who have no intention of returning to their country of origin, assimilate to the dominant culture of British and American democracy?)
*Goldberg, *Suicide of the West*, p. 322.

[43] Rose, p. 293.

emotional offense, they will not be equipped to defend themselves in the real world, having not been challenged to grow into mature human beings able to make a difference in the world.

Yet, it was at UC Berkeley, the home of "Free Speech," that Mario Savio, in the name of free speech, in 1964, convinced students to strike, to "put their bodies upon the gears" to shut down the university. At the time, students wanted to hear conflicting opinions, whereas the university thought its duty was to protect them, the opposite of today.

It's time for the university, the apex of learning, to retake the lead and jam the gears of political correctness. A free and open society, by definition, is not an environment free of conflicting opinions.

Free speech is integral to democracy. It provides instant information with respect to antidemocratic behavior—a rosebush before a vineyard, a canary in a mineshaft. It warns of imminent danger. Why, although today's news media is so diluted by entertainment and gossip, and despite the fears of its writing staff—the news media is not censored.[44]

Free speech is to democracy what price signals are to an economy: instant transmission of pertinent information. Price signals before the 2008 financial crisis revealed the folly of government having pressured banks to make subprime loans. Businesses may provide useless, even fraudulent goods and services, which is why consumers ask for government regulation (unaware, however, that government is usually the cause of economic crises), but we do not censor price signals.[45]

---

[44] Every article in the *New York Times*, from election day 2016 to election day 2020, was a direct or indirect attempt to *get that man out of office*. And from January 2021, to *keep* him out of office.

[45] Political reality in a democracy is that politicians are elected to regulate the economy and to extract revenue from the government (which extracted it from citizens) to deliver to their constituents. (Continued on next page)

A less utilitarian argument for free speech is the Jeffersonian notion that the basis for American democracy is that people can and do think for themselves—why citizens must hear all the arguments.

Can free speech go too far? Can tolerance of intolerance go too far? In the 20th century, the West tolerated communism, but at least communism advocated human rights. In the 21st century, the West tolerates Islam, but Islam does not advocate human rights. To the contrary, it finds Western freedoms repulsive. Muslims would cancel those freedoms, as their terrorists continually demonstrate.

To stand up to Islam, to challenge it, is one of the challenges of our time. We must not do as Europe did in the 1930s—not stand up to Hitler. If we do not defend ourselves, Islam, a non-Western civilization, soon to be an out-of-control nuclear threat, may very well sacrifice human life for what it believes is a greater good.[46]

(Continued from previous page) Demand that government stop taxing, censoring and spending, and you will not be reelected.

Dictatorship eliminates this problem. A benevolent and wise dictator simply decrees the correct solutions to societal problems—in the case of health care, for example, to cut *every* aspect of government intervention in that market. Cut Medicare! Why? Because price would drop 66 percent.

Except that there is no assurance a dictator or his or her successor will be wise and benevolent. That is why we have democracy: to vote leaders in or out.

Communism is an interesting alternative. For the history of mankind, stronger civilizations wiped out weaker ones, but communism, a weaker civilization, wiped out stronger ones. The uneducated replaced the educated. Witness the Chinese and Cambodian Cultural Revolutions. Or Cuba, where workers earning $1,000 a year replaced industrialists and business owners, their employers, earning $50,000 a year.

The attraction to communism is psychological freedom—where all citizens are fully employed, receive health care, education, cultural access, and pensions at retirement— which is why communism *will* make a comeback. Next time less dictatorial, but as soon as confiscated property and capital wear out, as soon as social and political freedom wither, it will collapse again. As did Hillary Clinton, who lost her bid for the U.S. presidency running on a collapsed platform of European socialism, the world will ask, "What happened?"

[46] Iran frequently brags that in a nuclear war with Israel, both (Continued on next page)

Economic Freedom

Classical liberalism is a genuine position. As progressive liberals demand social and political freedom, so, too, do classical liberals. But classical liberals also demand economic freedom. To a classical liberal, *there is nothing the market cannot provide*—why government should not intervene in the affairs of its citizens.[47]

The market order, however, has a serious philosophic problem. It doesn't seem natural. A human construct, it will always be refuted, according to historian Jonah Goldberg, by anti-capitalist political ideology, always some variant of the idea that society should operate like a family, a tribe, a community where everyone knows each other.[48]

Except,

> [E]very kind of totalitarian regime or authoritarian regime tries to take the values of the microcosm and apply them to the macrocosm. Nazism is tribalism for one race; fascism is tribalism for one country; communism is tribalism for one class. [T]ake those notions of social solidarity and intimacy from the microcosm and apply them to the macrocosm, and . . . you destroy liberty and the rule of law.[49]

The reverse is also wrong.

> [W]hen you take the logic of the macrocosm and you apply it to the microcosm, you destroy the engines of value generation that make society work. If you tried to turn a family into a business, it would ruin the family. If you tried

---

(Continued from previous page) countries would be annihilated, but Iran, whose population is ten times that of Israel, would have millions left over. "We won!" China may feel that way about Taiwan.

[47] There are a few things society may not want the market to provide, such as national defense, not because the market cannot provide it, but because society wants it provided by a neutral third party.

[48] Jonah Goldberg, *Suicide of the West*, p. 64.

[49] Nick Gillespie, "The Tribe of Liberty," Jonah Goldberg interview, *Reason*, October 2018, p. 53.

to make a country of 310 million people operate as if the president were our father or our mother, it would ruin everything [the nation] stands for.[50]

Still, according to Goldberg, this is exactly how all backward countries operate: tribal—where favoritism, nepotism, self-dealing, patronizing and graft are perfectly acceptable politics.[51]

This is why advocates of social and economic justice, Marxism 1848, believe free societies favor the privileged: because in societies where individuals pursue their interests without government regulation, only the privileged survive. Not true! Life doesn't work that way. Man, an animal in nature, survives by pursuing his self-interest—which is to survive. Unregulated society, free markets—all are a product of centuries of self-organization and self-correction. All evolved, as did life in the universe, as a product of trial and error. Social, political and economic freedom were not designed. Restraint was designed. A bad idea.

But people are different, have different professions, have different values. That is the reason to have a free society.

A free society has extreme differences in compensation, in pay, because in free-market economies, earnings are a function of subjective demand for a produced product, not the value of time, effort or materials involved in its production. In a market economy, as income and wealth are unrelated, so too are income and labor unrelated.[52]

To believe otherwise (Marxist labor theory of value) is a huge mistake. In free-market economies, workers in an industry may very well not earn enough to purchase the product they manufacture. To the contrary, where there is large demand to be in a profession, wage is at its lowest (unless a union or guild artificially restricts entry, as the American Medical Association restricts entry into the medical profession—to keep salaries high). Historically, salaries for

---

[50] Gillespie, p. 53.

[51] Goldberg, *Suicide of the* West, p. 64.

[52] For a full discussion of the idea that income and wealth are two separate matters, please read David Parker, *Income and Wealth* (Waterside Productions, 2021).

professional athletes were lower than school teachers'—because demand to play professional sports is always higher than the supply of openings on professional teams. True in the arts or any career requiring long preparation and dedication. Athletes and artists would play for free if that was the only way they could perform. Prepare a lifetime to play Hamlet, then turn down the opportunity because it doesn't pay enough? Never. It is because professional sports and acting are broadcast on television that salaries are high.[53]

In other words, in a free economy, demand for economic and social justice is nonsense. The rich are not rich at the expense of the poor. That's Marxism. According to F. A. Hayek, the demand for economic equality is the tribal instinct resurfacing, a nostalgic atavism for a tribal past, with its loyalties and jealousies.

> When all of your identity is bound up in a single group or cause, your concern for institutions and people outside of your group diminishes or vanishes.
>
> An open society is one where we have many allegiances— to family and society, to work and faith, etc. When you have competing or simply multiple allegiance, you open yourself up to the idea that opponents are not enemies. Pluralism creates social and psychological spaces where others are free to pursue their interest too. In an open society . . . the African-American policeman counts white officers as fellow brothers of the badge.[54]

In this way, pluralism, federalism, are a protection for democracy. They are a guard against one group dictating national agenda.

---

[53] A 19-year-old baseball player does not negotiate his salary. His agent does. His agent asks one question: What percent of the team's multimillion-dollar revenue will his client generate? Salary is a percent of that revenue.

[54] *Goldberg, Suicide of the* West, p. 62. Note: The Founding Fathers knew their weaknesses, knew that slavery was immoral. It is why they created the U.S. Constitution: to restrain *their* excesses. They knew the Constitution would lead to freeing the slaves, that the political situation *at the time* dictated compromise, not settling the issue of slavery, yet. The choice was slavery and the Constitution or no slavery and no Constitution. Exhausted from the Revolutionary War, America was not ready to fight its civil war. (Continued on next page)

This San Francisco conservative lives in a multicultural world. My friends, family, members of my jazz sextet, all are of diverse racial and ethnic backgrounds. I prefer that environment. I am a card-carrying member of the ACLU precisely because that organization unequivocally defends free speech and political freedom (or used to[55]), yet wonder why the ACLU doesn't defend economic freedom. It should, because in a Jeffersonian democracy, citizens, including those in business, can be trusted to act morally. Don't underestimate the self-correction process of nature, of markets, of the American citizen.[56]

Europeans trust neither citizens nor the market. To a European, the very purpose of government, nay, civilization, is to protect citizens from the market—and from themselves. Europeans

---

(Continued from previous page)

The anti-slavery movement has little to entitle it to being called a new thing under the sun . . . The patriots of the American Revolution clearly saw, and with all their inconsistency, they had the grace to confess the abhorrent character of slavery, and to hopefully predict its overthrow and complete extirpation. Washington and Jefferson, Patrick Henry, and Luther Martin, Franklin, and Adams, Madison and Monroe, and a host of earnest statesmen, jurists, scholars and divines of the country, were among those who looked forward to this happy consumption.

—Frederick Douglass*

*Philip S. Foner, ed., *Frederick Douglass: Selected Speeches and Writings* (Chicago Review Press, 1999), p. 31, as cited by David Horowitz, *Black Book*, p. 98. Horowitz comments that Douglass' view connects the destiny of liberated slaves to America's own aspirations as a nation.

God who gave us life gave us liberty. Can the liberties of a nation be secure when we have removed a conviction that these liberties are the gift of God? Indeed, I tremble for my country when I reflect that God is just, that his justice cannot sleep forever. Commerce between master and slave is despotism. Nothing is more certainly written in the book of fate than that these people are to be free.

—Jefferson Memorial

[55] Today the ACLU protects the right not to hear free speech, the right to cancel speech. Today, according to its current leadership (to the dismay of its past leaders), the ACLU's core mission is to defend progressivism. From 2016 to 2020, to unseat Donald Trump.

[56] And don't underestimate today's authoritarian leaders. Xi Jinping, Vladimir Putin, Recep Erdogan, master strategists—firmly in control of their populations, peoples with no history of individual liberty who seem not to object—are destroying every aspect of democracy in each of their countries. If no one rebels, if those countries kowtow, those leaders will represent the future of authoritarianism. Good luck, Hong Kong. A generation of your young face suppression and imprisonment.

will always exchange freedom for security, and pay the price. Not in the habit of monitoring freedom or monitoring government, between 1870 and 1945, Europeans did not prevent three enormous devastations—the Franco-Prussian War, World War I, World War II —a perfect example of this writer's message: social, political and economic freedom are so inherently interconnected that the extent to which a nation loses one of those freedoms is the extent to which it loses the other two, why those wars were fought: to regain lost freedoms.[57]

Conservatives view with repugnance progressives' willingness under the banner of pragmatism to compromise freedom, to appease forces demanding economic and social equality at the expense of adhering to the Constitution, in that moving forward from the Constitution *is* the definition of progressivism. To conservatives, government is not a vehicle for citizens to satisfy personal goals such as racial and ethnic diversity, a man on the moon, subsidies of industries, zero emission of carbon dioxide. Racial and ethnic diversity are not goals; they are reality.[58] To force children onto busses to integrate schools runs roughshod over freedom. A deeply free people, American parents pulled their children from those schools. In free societies, citizens always find a way to circumvent restraint.[59]

The lesson: don't engineer a free society. Don't use the political process to rectify past evils (except to remove laws that made those evils possible). Enforce basic rules: The U.S. Constitution, the Bill of Rights. Considering the history of racial

---

[57] The European Union (EU), however, is not about freedom; it is about control. The European Union, European socialism, is so far removed from British classical liberalism that Britain finally decided to leave.

[58] Before the Civil Rights Act of 1968, discrimination in housing prevented diversity. After the Act, the situation barely changed—by choice.

[59] Between 1970 and 2000, one at a time, American parents pulled their children from the public schools—*the* reason American public schools today are failing; there's no one left. Public housing, public schools, public prisons, that's what's left. Note: many parents wanted integration to succeed and waited before pulling their children—until gradually, parents *and* teachers realized the schools were no longer working. (This author did not pull his kids, although he made certain they were enrolled in those very few schools that upheld standards. In San Francisco, 10 out of 100.)

discrimination in the U.S., yes, for a limited period there could be laws that forbid discrimination and promote affirmative action in hiring and school enrollment. But, *for a limited period*, say 100 years, 1968 to 2068—after which, like freedom of hate speech formerly defended by the ACLU, freedom of loving discrimination, the right to associate with those whom one chooses, must again be defended. It's a price of freedom.

––––––––

Engineer a free society? That's socialism. The danger: relaxation of vigilance in the defense of individual liberty, loss of ability to recognize threats to freedom, including economic freedom. That is why there was no opposition to forming the European Union, Germany's grand scheme for economic dominance of Europe. Not paying attention, Europeans let Germany, under guise of the humanitarian goal of preventing future wars, pull a fast one. As China is conquering South Asia (at least economically), Germany is conquering Europe (economically). Its weapon: The euro.

Who created the euro? Germany: to get rid of the deutsche mark, its overvalued currency. Then, trap Europe. The lower-valued euro lowered the price of German exports—enough to create a balance of payments problem for the rest of Europe (which imports more goods from Germany than it exports to Germany). To pay for that surplus of imports, those nations need more euros, the demand for which causes the price of the euro to rise. With a higher-priced euro, all of Europe, except Germany, is, then, less competitive on the world market. As Greece gave away its domestic currency (the drachma), so, too, did most European countries. Those nations are trapped, because Germany will never let the euro be devalued. Germany would be throwing away the weapon, in conjunction with its efficient manufacturing, that allows it to control Europe.

Automobiles are a good example. German automobiles outsell European *and* American automobiles. As a $50,000 Cadillac cannot compete with its equivalent $40,000 Mercedes-Benz, Germany (and Japan) have decimated the American auto industry (except Tesla, which is now larger than Ford, GM, and Chrysler combined). The European and American auto industries survive today only because they are subsidized.[60] [61]

Greece will *never* manufacture Mercedes-Benzes. Greece's price to the market would be double Germany's. Zorba the Greek is not Hans the Hun. Before the euro, Greece could have devalued its currency, the drachma, and perhaps competed, but Germany took that currency away. Trapped in the euro, Greece may be permanently trapped in high unemployment. According to Pew Research Center, unemployment in Greece was 19.3 percent in 2018, down from 27.5 percent in 2013.[62] All of Europe, including Germany, is trapped in the euro. Overvalued, it is why unemployment in Europe (except Germany) is higher than in the U.S.

In the 1920s and '30s, Germany took away guns from all citizens (the excuse: the carnage of World War I), which in the 1940s, allowed German Nazis to round up their victims, without resistance. Today, Germany has taken away European currencies from most citizens (the excuse, which is the reason for the European Union, to prevent another world war), which allows efficient German manufacturing to devour another victim, the economies of Europe, without resistance.[63]

Then, as the EU controls Europe's borders, so, too, Germany controls those borders—why it was able to persuade Europe to do

---

[60] Note also that over and above the nation's budget deficit and national debt, the U.S. has unfunded liabilities of $123 trillion. That $123 trillion guarantees not only Social Security and Medicare, both of which today are paid for by borrowing, it also guarantees the nation's private pension funds, General Motors', for example, which, like most corporations, spend rather than set aside those funds.

[61] In other words, to purchase an automobile: save for the down payment, make the monthly payments, add five percent to your income taxes. In America, that five percent is your charitable donation to General Motors.

[62] Kat Devlin, "How Unemployment Rates Relate to Economic Attitudes in the EU," *Pew Research Organization*, December 11, 2019, https://www.pewresearch.org/fact-tank/2019/12/11/how-unemployment-rates-relate-to-economic-attitudes-in-the-eu/.

[63] From 1941 to 1945, had Germany welcomed rather than eliminated its Jews, Germany might have controlled the world: economically, financially, militarily, and, with nuclear weapons. The fact, however, that Germany did what it did must not be forgotten. As the Mafia have no regard for human life—killing in their mind is a business, not a personal decision—so too Germans and today, mainland Chinese. (Continued on next page)

the "humanitarian" thing: take in unlimited immigration from the war-torn Middle East. However, the extent to which Germany takes the majority of those immigrants, apprenticing them in "the German way," further strengthens its manufacturing in relation to the rest of Europe. The backlash may be very unpleasant. Since World War II, after a painstaking effort to build democracies in Europe, such immigration is rekindling xenophobic and racist discourse. This time the scapegoat will be immigration.[64]

> We have to return to a time when Italians believed in a state that guarantees security, order and legality.
>
> Out-of-control immigration brought chaos, rage and social clashes.[65]

(Continued from previous page) Nations with no regard for human life and no fear of war have an advantage that must not be ignored.

The cold, calculated indifference that allowed Germans to gas alive six million Jews is the same indifference in 2015 with which Volkswagen created an automobile that spewed 40 times the level of nitrogen oxide allowed by the Clean Air Act.* That indifference will again be unleashed if latent Prussian militarism is again allowed to flower—should American-led NATO remove its troops [200,000 until 1990, 35,000 today. Ditto Japan.** 350,000 troops, 55,000 today. Afghanistan, 13,000 in 2019, 2,500 early 2021.].

*Nitrogen oxide is not Zyklon B, but one SS doctor described what he saw: shouting and screaming of the victims could be heard through the opening and it was clear that they fought for their lives. If the gas chamber had been crowded, which they typically were, the corpses were found half-squatting, their skin discolored pink with red and green spots, with some found foaming at their mouths, or bleeding from their ears. www.quora.com, "What Would It Be Like to Die of Exposure to Zyklon B?"

**Nanjing. Batches of Chinese civilians were rounded up and herded into slaughter pits. Here the grinning Japanese soldiers would either bury them alive, hack them to death with their swords, use them for bayonet practice, or pour petrol on the victims and burn them alive. The bodies of thousands of victims of the slaughter were dumped into the Yangtze River until the river was red with their blood. After looting Nanking of anything of value, the Japanese started fires that gutted one third of the city. Total dead: 300,000. "A Small Cross-section of Japanese War Crimes," www.pacificwar.org,
https://www.pacificwar.org.au/JapWarCrimes/TenWarCrimes/Rape_Nanking.html.

[64] *Es gibt noch Juden in Deutschland?* —posted at a Jewish museum in Berlin. [There are still Jews in Germany?] Hey, let's get the Muslims now!

[65] James Politi and Davide Ghiglione, "Meloni Takes Italian Far-Right Back to 1930s Roots," *Financial Times*, February 9, 2018, https://www.ft.com/content/f8c32044-0d92-11e8-8eb7-42f857ea9f09. [Meloni was accompanied by Rachele Mussolini, Mussolini's daughter.]

That's the rhetoric. When there is widespread disaffection with traditional political parties because those parties don't stand for anything, thus, don't do anything, *that* leads to support for the far right—Austria, Poland, Hungary, Czech Republic, Italy, France, Donald Trump in the U.S.

In Europe, such populism always unleashes anti-Semitism.

> The French still struggle with it as they try, for example, not to recognize two of their greatest writers, Charles Maurras and Louis-Ferdinand Céline, virulent anti-Semites who were condemned as traitors for having collaborated with the Nazi invasion. The French long held back from recognizing them because France recognizes that it would give those authors too much moral authority. To Maurras, for example (and to many who are still monarchist Catholic traditional conservative), Jews, Protestants, Freemasons and immigrants are responsible for the French Revolution, the single biggest historical disaster and permanent threat to the nation.[66]

To Sudhir Hazareesingh, author of *How the French Think*, the question itself is very French:

> In any other democracy, the status of someone like Maurras would just be a matter of debate among historians. The French Republic has developed a habit of using history to orient collective memory, legitimize its power, and ensure social cohesion.[67]

Well, there it is: postmodernism opening the door to anti-Semitism, to far-right populism, to the manipulation of public opinion with its declaring of all points of view legitimate. It is European multiculturalists "using history to orient collective memory to legitimize power, to ensure social cohesion." Beware the backlash!

---

[66] Anne-Sylvaine Chassany, "France's Intellectual Anti-Semitism Debate Opens Old Wounds," *Financial* Times, February 9, 2018, https://www.ft.com/content/a3b8029a-0be9-11e8-8eb7-42f857ea9f09.

[67] Chassany, *Financial Times.*

In 1900, Zionists started returning to Palestine, a land of desert malaria-infested swamps, millennially present nomads, and scattered properties barely worth owning (whose landlords lived in Alexandria and Damascus). Yet, thanks to those Zionists, for the first time in centuries, there was employment in the Middle East. Arabs from throughout the Middle East began immigrating to Palestine. Their population soon matched then exceeded the Zionists—after which the Arabs claimed the Zionists were taking their land. Arab tribal instincts led to pogroms of the Israeli settlements, and after 1948 (Israel's creation), to bombing of cafés and school busses—all perfectly understandable to multiculturalists who claim that people in less developed countries must defend themselves by any means necessary and be defended from the colonial instincts of their more developed neighbors. Free Palestine! Boycott Israel![68]

[68] Note: with the creation of Israel in 1948, followed by three wars to undo that creation, 500,000 Jews were expelled from throughout the Middle East. They moved to Israel. Of course they took some Palestinian land. They had to live somewhere.

It is not the fault of Israelis that Palestinians cannot live in peace with them. Jews are a peaceful people (except when they defend themselves), whereas Iraq, for example, with the largest middle class in the Middle East, after the U.S. rid it of Saddam Hussein, could not resist returning to violence to solve its problems, just as after the Arab Spring most Middle Eastern nations returned to violence—contained only with the reinstallation of military dictatorships.

3

SAN FRANCISCO

A San Francisco Conservative

A San Francisco conservative: to those on the Left, an oxymoron—it's not possible; to those on the Right, a sigh of relief—we're not alone!

Who is a San Francisco conservative? Someone not *that* conservative. This author. A classical liberal, not socially conservative. Politically conservative, I believe the U.S. Constitution should be interpreted literally—that a nation that can't abide by a simple set of rules written on ONE page doesn't deserve to exist. Economically conservative: I believe the market, not government, should solve a nation's economic problems. A classical liberal, I understand that social, political and economic freedom are so inherently interconnected that society cannot restrict one without restricting the other two. Why restrict any of them?

What are we so afraid of? This author, a card-carrying member of the ACLU, wishes that organization, à la the late Supreme Court Justice Antonin Scalia, would defend economic freedom as it defends social and political freedom, as it defends free speech. Why do San Francisco liberals balk at economic freedom? Creative business, creative teaching, creative art—none of these demand government regulation. As humans are a part of nature, so too are their constructs—why nature's invisible hand will spontaneously correct for their excesses.

But what is government itself, but the greatest of all reflections on human nature?   If men were angels, no government would be necessary. If angels were to govern men, neither external nor internal controls on government would be necessary. In framing a government which is to be administered by men over men, the great difficulty lies in this: you must first enable the government to control the governed; and in the next place oblige it to control itself. A dependence on the people is, no doubt, the primary control on the government; but experience has taught mankind the necessity of auxiliary precautions [why we have checks and balances in government].

—*The Federalist Papers, No. 51* (James Madison)

Look at minimum wage: a political solution to an economic problem. Why do politicians and government underestimate citizens? Workers never work for less than a subsistence wage. During the Industrial Revolution, during the Great Depression, workers were never paid less than subsistence wage. Outside the occasional downturn, the Achilles' heel of a dynamic economy is that there is always a labor shortage. This is why wages are always bid up and why the U.S. looks the other way with respect to illegal immigration: we need those workers. Why wages in China will soon match those in Europe, the U.S., Japan and South Korea: China has a dynamic economy. Already China has a labor shortage in mid-level management and above; those wages are double that of the nation.[1]

Why does France always have high unemployment? Because France has a less-than-dynamic economy. During the 2008 Great Recession there were advertisements in the Paris Metro, *in English*, screaming: "50,000 jobs available in the U.S. Come to America!"[2]

---

[1] "Wages of mid- and above-level management rose 10 percent from 2018 to 2019, and are now twice the wage level of all employees. See National Bureau of Statistics of China, "Average Annual Wage of Employed Persons in Different Positions," May 18, 2020, http://www.stats.gov.cn/english/PressRelease/202105/t20210520_1817731.html.

[2] With that century-on-century message, "Come to America," the U.S. built a world-class population: four million in 1790, 330 million today. The U.S. robbed and continues to rob the world of its most ambitious citizens.

Look at rent control: a political solution to an economic problem. San Francisco doesn't have high rent; it has a housing shortage, an economic problem, for which the city chose a political solution: rent control. Supported by a host of laws, San Francisco tells its landlords what they cannot do and cannot say to their tenants: literally, they do not have the right to negotiate with each other.[3] Rent control, a taking of social, political and economic freedom, the basis of a free society, is a violation of the 5th Amendment.[4] The real solution, the economic solution, is to build more housing: 300,000 units, immediately.[5]

———

Solving social and economic problems through the political process ignores an underlying truth; namely, no one can do for others what they must do for themselves. Short-term relief, even rent control, may be necessary, but long-term, it undermines the ability of human beings to adjust. Humans are not stupid. If not smart, they're at least clever—why, for example, neither the rich nor poor pay taxes, reason alone for government to stop trying to solve their problems.

Look at the War on Poverty: it failed its goals. Poverty was 15 percent in 1965 and remained 15 percent every year thereafter.

---

[3] In January 2004, the San Francisco Board of Supervisors announced: "Except in a public safety emergency even casual verbal discussion between landlord and tenant is harassment of the tenant." A landlord asking, "How are you doing today?" is construed to mean, "Are you healthy enough to still reside in the apartment? When are you leaving?" In San Francisco, communication between landlord and tenant is through attorneys. See Chapter 3, "Landlord Documents."

[4] No person shall be deprived of life, liberty or property without due process of law; nor shall private property be taken for public use without just compensation.

[5] That will never happen. Neither tenants nor landlords are asking for it. Under rent control, both are way ahead. With constriction on *supply* coupled with a continually increasing population, *demand* (as the San Francisco Bay Area is a major center for all future industry: artificial intelligence, biological engineering, nanotechnology, space exploration), housing appreciates in value far in excess of the loss of revenue from lower rent. [Investment tip: purchase real estate in rent-controlled cities. The rate of return exceeds most other investments.]

On average, the rate never dropped.[6] Remove those social programs now, and poverty jumps to 22 percent. The increase is what Charles Murray calls latent poverty.[7] Worse, the War on Poverty reversed the previous ten-year downward trend out of poverty.[8]

Minimum wage, rent control, the War on Poverty, why do progressives believe there are no consequences to government intervention in people's lives? Ignorant of the laws of money and economics, with an elitist fear and underestimation of the masses, of course they believe that citizens are not capable of thinking and acting for themselves, why they need government protection—a thought as un-American as it gets. Worse, progressives really believe government can tax the rich—the only solution progressives have ever offered. Naïve. The rich have nowhere near the money to pay off the nation's yearly budget deficit (certainly not the $28 trillion national debt), most of which is for social services.[9] Even if they did, outside of socialism, government will never collect it. Apple may talk "green" and "diversity," but 94 percent of its wealth is offshore, and its headquarters are in Ireland; Apple has no intention of paying taxes.[10]

---

[6] U.S. Census Bureau, "Historical Poverty Tables: People and Families—1959 to 2019, https://www.census.gov/data/tables/time-series/demo/income-poverty/historical-poverty-people.html.

[7] Charles Murray, *Losing Ground: American Social Policy 1950-1980* (Basic Books, 1984), p. 65.

[8] Murray, p. 57.

[9] U.S. Treasury, U.S. National Debt Clock, usdebtclock.org.

[10] Corporate tax in America at the time of Apple's relocation was 39 percent, the highest in the world. Under Donald Trump, 25 percent. In Ireland, 15 percent.

Progressivism

> Conservatives beware: If the main elements in [President] Joe Biden's American Family Plan become law, they'll be very hard to repeal. Why? Because they'll deliver huge, indeed trans-formational benefits to millions.
>
> —Paul Krugman[11]

In his 1964 State of the Union address, in the midst of the Vietnam War with the nation on a wartime deficit economy, President Lyndon B. Johnson proclaimed, "This administration today, here and now, declares unconditional war on poverty in America." "The richest nation on earth can afford to win it." Extending Franklin D. Roosevelt's New Deal, Johnson added funding for food, housing, education, job training, family welfare, health care for seniors (Medicare) and health care for the poor (Medicaid). "Our aim is not only to relieve the symptoms of poverty, but to cure it and, above all, to prevent it."[12]

Except, the War on Poverty is paid for by borrowing—although that is not the real problem. Americans always pay by borrowing.[13] The real problem is that the nation's government is trying to do something governments cannot do: provide for rather than protect life, liberty and property. The War on Poverty failed because social and economic problems cannot be solved through the political process, by throwing money at them. As overheard in a Brooklyn barbershop: "If you can solve a problem by throwing money at it, you don't have a problem."

---

[11] Paul Krugman, "Good Luck to Republicans if Biden's Family Plan Becomes Law," Opinion Page, *New York Times*, April 30, 2021, https://www.nytimes.com/2021/04/29/opinion/child-care-biden.html.

[12] President Johnson's State of the Union address, January 8, 1964, https://www.americanrhetoric.com/speeches/lbj1964stateoftheunion.htm.

[13] Socialism in Europe is also paid for by borrowing—but at least Europeans acknowledge that socialism requires a 50 percent tax rate. They don't protest because they don't see that 50 percent on their tax returns. They see 25 percent, plus 25 percent as a regressive value-added tax on the sale of all goods and services they purchase.

Correct. Social problems are personal problems. They stem from human nature: laziness, not getting an education, not acquiring a job skill—something money cannot remedy. That small percentage of the population too mentally or physically disabled to work is not the problem; money *can* solve that. That population, in a market economy, is provided for by charity. Consider: *Every year in America, 260,000 millionaires die.* If they didn't pay taxes when they were alive (which they probably didn't), they pay then.[14]

Together, the New Deal and the War on Poverty have created an intergenerationally dependent nation. We are losing what in 1835 Alexis de Tocqueville most admired about America: our self-reliance —which he acknowledged was missing in Europe—although in their own way, today's millennials are self-reliant. They seemingly feel no anxiety about health care or retirement: they know they will inherit from their parents, the richest generation this nation ever produced.

The New Deal, the War on Poverty, President Biden's American Family Plan—their underlying assumption is that social and economic problems can be solved by spending money. The title of Krugman's Op-Ed is, "Good Luck to Republicans if Biden's Family Plan Becomes Law." But *it's not for government to create jobs*; it's for the private sector, the market. It's simply unconstitutional for government to do that. Only in a democracy can citizens ask for such a thing. But the U.S. is not a democracy! We're a *constitutional* democracy. Citizens cannot just vote 90 to 10 to do something illegal, for example, allow government to improve the economy by providing "transformational benefits for the nation" (per Krugman's opening quote). Plus, there is no need for that. In a dynamic economy, apart from a downturn, there is always a labor shortage.

---

[14] According to Global Wealth Report 2020 by Credit Suisse, eight percent of Americans are millionaires, https://www.cnbc.com/2021/02/09/more-than-8-percent-of-american-adults-are-millionaires-heres-how-they-got-wealthy. Eight percent of 330 million is 26 million. With a death rate in the U.S. of one percent, 260,000 millionaires die every year. If estate tax is 40 percent, tax revenue is $1 trillion *per year* (260,000 x $1,000,000 = $2.6 trillion x .40 = $1.04 trillion). Eight percent seems high, so, cut it in half. $500 billion a year.

Government has no business being involved. Government can encourage economic growth because economic growth means increased standard of living, for everyone, but government has no business providing social and financial security at the expense of individual liberty. That's how dictators ride into office—by offering social and financial security in exchange for remaining in power: Bismarck, Hitler, Mussolini. Today, Xi, Putin, Erdogan. National Socialism.

At the start of the American Revolution, Thomas Jefferson declared: "If you're afraid of democracy, leave. If you're afraid to live without a king or a queen, afraid to give every person the vote, afraid to live without big government, leave." Thousands did. They fled to Canada. Were he living then, Krugman would have fled.

His closing argument:

> And if these plans improve life for millions of Americans, will anyone besides professional ideologues care if they're "big government"?[15]

Yikes, will anyone care if we throw out the Constitution? That's what big government means. That's what the 2024 election will be about.

Excerpts from President Johnson's State of the Union Speech January 8, 1964:[16]

---

[15] Krugman, "Good Luck to Republicans if Biden's Family Plan Becomes Law" (cited earlier). Yes, government can create jobs, or give money to employers in exchange for hiring more employees, but the nation loses more than it gains. As cited in David Parker, *Income and Wealth*, "Trade," (Waterside Productions, 2021), p. 25-26, the cost of protecting a single job by a tariff is approximately $500,000 in lost national revenue. Politicians Left and Right approve tariffs for one reason: "protecting American jobs" gets them elected.

[16] Lyndon Baines Johnson, "First State of the Union Address," January 8, 1984, American Rhetoric Online Speech Bank, https://www.americanrhetoric.com/speeches/lbj1964stateoftheunion.htm.

Let this session of Congress be known as the session which did more for civil rights than the last hundred sessions combined; as the session which enacted the most far- reaching tax cut of our time; as the session which declared all-out war on human poverty and unemployment in these United States; as the session which finally recognized the health needs of all our older citizens; as the session which reformed our tangled transportation and transit policies; as the session which achieved the most effective, efficient foreign aid program ever; and as the session which helped to build more homes, more schools, more libraries, and more hospitals than any single session of Congress in the history of our Republic.

[If you believe this, you are a progressive. It's pure socialism. Not only has the cost of the War on Poverty amounted to more than three times the expense of all U.S. military wars since the American Revolution, $23 trillion, but the war has been lost.[17] Consider housing projects: torn down as unlivable—because they were planned by government rather than by professional developers; public school test scores: the lowest in the world for the last 50 years (why the U.S. Department of Education claims that only 36 percent of the nation tests proficient in reading and math when previously test scores for American public schools were among the highest[18]); and the cost of health care: highest in the world—thanks to Medicare.]

All this and more can and must be done. It can be done by this summer, and it can be done without any increase in spending. In fact, under the budget that I shall shortly submit, it can be done with an actual reduction in Federal expenditures and Federal employment. [Reader, I hope you don't believe this.]

---

[17] Rachel Sheffield and Robert Rector, "The War on Poverty After 50 years," The Heritage Foundation, September 9, 2014, cites $22 trillion (https://www.heritage.org/poverty-and-inequality/report/the-war-poverty-after-50-years). Another reference, *Inside Sources*, cites $23 trillion, March 14, 2021.

[18] "Proficient" is a euphemism for D+.

This administration today, here and now, declares unconditional war on poverty in America. I urge this Congress and all Americans to join with me in that effort.

It will not be a short or easy struggle, no single weapon or strategy will suffice, but we shall not rest until that war is won. The richest Nation on earth can afford to win it. We cannot afford to lose it. One thousand dollars invested in salvaging an unemployable youth today can return $40,000 or more in his lifetime.

[This *is* Paul Krugman's argument for the American Family Planning Act: create jobs.]

Our aim is not only to relieve the symptom of poverty, but to cure it and, above all, to prevent it. No single piece of legislation, however, is going to suffice.

Very often a lack of jobs and money is not the cause of poverty, but the symptom. The cause may lie deeper in our failure to give our fellow citizens a fair chance to develop their own capacities, in a lack of education and training, in a lack of medical care and housing, in lack of decent communities in which to live and bring up their children.

[Immigrants from Africa are drowning at sea to come here. Immigrants from Latin America are dying of asphyxiation in closed trucks sneaking across the border to come here. *They* know what Americans do not, that "education and training and medical care and housing and decent communities to live in and bring up children are *precisely* what this nation has to offer.]

The program I shall propose will emphasize this cooperative approach to help that one-fifth of all American families with incomes too small to even meet their basic needs.

[One-fifth is 20 percent. No, the U.S. Census Bureau reports that poverty since 1959 has remained on average 15 percent. And nowhere in Johnson's address is a distinction made between relative and absolute poverty, that in America, the bottom five percent live better than 95 percent of the rest of the world. As President Biden's American Family Planning Act is political grandstanding, so too was President Johnson's War on Poverty and Franklin Roosevelt's New Deal—an appeal to emotion rather than to reason. Politics!]

When you can measure what you're talking about, express it in numbers; only then can you say you know something. If you can't measure or express it in numbers, your knowledge is unsatisfactory. At best, it is the beginning of knowledge.

As proposed in President Johnson's 1964 Inaugural address, the War on Poverty would cost *nothing*. Sounded good. Where were the numbers? As televangelism makes God an instrument of instant gratification, so, too, politics makes our political parties an instrument of instant gratification, in which God is replaced by spending: "the solution to our problems."

"No numbers" is the heart of progressivism—where programs are never tested before implementation. Karl Marx himself said that communism was so new, so absolutely without historical precedent, that we cannot know in advance how it will turn out.[19] Yet socialists and communists are satisfied with that explanation—based on the German philosopher Hegel, who said that every 1,000 years or so mankind, collectively, makes an evolutionary leap. To Marxists, communism was that leap, the understanding that the economy determines citizens' social and political relations, that man's misery, a function of the economy, can be eliminated by eliminating private property and private ownership of the means of production: Utopia.

Marx was correct. The economic system does determine social and political relations. But why wouldn't a free economy create free social and political relations? The controlled economies

---

[19] Trying to convince Congress to pass the Affordable Care Act, House Speaker Nancy Pelosi pleaded:

> "It's going to be very, very exciting. [Congress] has to pass the bill so that you can find out what's in it, away from the fog of controversy."—Nancy Pelosi, March 9, 2010, at the Legislative Conference for the National Association of Counties.

of the Soviet Union, China, Cambodia, Cuba, North Korea, socialism from the Left, communism, coupled with the controlled economies of Germany, Italy and Japan in the 1930s and '40s, socialism from the right, fascism, together, certainly did not create social and political freedom. They created an epithet for the 20th century:

Socialism: 100 Million Murdered

For the U.S.:

The War on Poverty: $23 trillion debt

———

The close of the Soviet drama was unpredicted because the very nature of the Soviet Union was without precedent. It was not an organic development but an artificial creation —the first society in history to be dreamed up by intellectuals and constructed according to plan. The crisis of Soviet society was not so much a traditional crisis of legitimacy and rule as it was the crisis of an *idea*—a monstrously wrong idea that had been imposed on society by an intellectual elite; an idea so passionately believed, and yet so profoundly mistaken, that it had caused more human misery and suffering than any single force in history before.[20]

[Progressivism, the New Deal, the War on Poverty, these, too, are an *idea* dreamt up and constructed according to plan.]

This suffering could not be justified by the augments of the left that the revolutionary changes were "at least an improvement on what existed before." Contrary to the progressive myth that radicals invented to justify their failures, Czarist Russia was not a merely pitiful, semi-barbaric state when the socialists seized power. By 1917,

---

[20] David Horowitz, *The Black Book of the American Left: The Collected Conservative Writings of David Horowitz* (Second Thoughts Books, 2017), p. 77.

Russia was already the fourth industrial power in the world. Its rail networks had tripled since 1890, and its industrial output had increased by three-quarters since the century began. Over half of all Russian children between eight and eleven years of age were enrolled in schools, while 68 percent of all military conscripts had been tested literate. A cultural renaissance was underway in dance, painting, literature and music; the names Blok, Kandinsky, Mayakovsky, Pasternak, Diaghilev, Rachmaninov and Stravinsky were already figures of world renown.[21]

[After the Revolution, Russia no longer produced figures of world renown.[22] Creative people need to live in a creative environment. A sad commentary on Left-wing intellectuals is that they do not know that creative artists have everything in common with creative industrialists, why artists work in creative centers of commerce: those in business want and need art, why they purchase it, whereas intellectuals and academics talk about art but don't purchase it; they purchase posters. Diego Rivera found his soulmates in Ford and Rockefeller, who in turn asked Rivera to paint the entire lobby of Rockefeller Center in New York City, the capitalist center of the world, knowing Rivera was a communist. Stupidly, Rivera placed a portrait of Lenin in the mural. Rockefeller asked him to remove it. Frida Kahlo told him to leave it. Rockefeller had the mural destroyed.]

In 1905, a constitutional monarchy with an elected parliament had been created in which freedom of the press, assembly and association were guaranteed, if not always observed. By 1917 legislation to create a welfare state, including the right to strike and provisions for workers' insurance was already in force; and before it was dissolved by Lenin's Bolsheviks, Russia's first truly democratic parliament had been convened.[23]

---

[21] Horowitz, p. 77.

[22] A few works did come out of the gulag.

[23] Horowitz, p. 77.

The Marxist Revolution destroyed all this, tearing the Russian people out of history's womb and robbing whole generations of their minimal birthright, the opportunity to struggle for a decent life.[24] Yet even as this political abortion was being completed and the nation was plunging into its deepest abyss, the very logic of revolution forced its leaders to expand their lie: to insist that the very nightmare they had created was indeed the kingdom of freedom and justice the revolution had promised.[25] [*Cf. Darkness at Noon*]

It is in this bottomless chasm between reality and promise that our one argument is finally joined. You [today's communists and socialists who believe that "next time it will be different"] seek to separate the terror-filled actualities of the Soviet experience from the magnificent harmonies of the social dream. But it is the dream itself that begets the reality, and requires the terror. This is the revolutionary paradox you want to ignore.[26]

Because of the nature of its political mission, this terror was immeasurably greater than the repression it replaced. Whereas the czarist police had several hundred agents at its height, the Bolshevik *Cheka* began its career with several hundred *thousand*. Whereas the czarist secret police had operated within the framework of a rule of law, the *Cheka* (and its successors) did not. The czarist police repressed extra-legal opponents of the political regime. To create the socialist future, the *Cheka* targeted whole social categories—regardless of individual behavior or attitude—for liquidation.[27]

The results were predictable. "Up until 1905," wrote Aleksandr Solzhenitsyn in his monumental record of the Soviet *gulag*, "the death penalty was an exceptional measure in Russia." From 1876 to 1904, 486 people were executed—17 people a year, for the whole country—a figure which included the executions of non-political

---

[24] Struggle for a decent life is the meaning of life: you get out of life what you put in. No effort, no joy.

[25] Horowitz, p. 78.

[26] Horowitz, p. 78.

[27] Horowitz, p. 79.

criminals. During the years of the 1905 revolution and its suppression, "the number of executions rocketed upward, astounding Russian imaginations, calling forth tears from Tolstoy [and] many others; from 1905 through 1908 about 2,200 persons were executed—forty-five a month. This, as Tagantsev said, was an *epidemic of executions*. It came to an abrupt end."[28]

But then came the Bolshevik seizure of power. "In a period of sixteen months (June 1918 to October 1919) more than sixteen thousand persons were shot, which is to say *more than one thousand a month*." These executions, carried out by the *Cheka* without trial and by revolutionary tribunals without due process, were executions of people exclusively accused of political crimes. And this was only a drop in the sea of executions to come. The true figures will never be known, but in the two years 1937 and 1938, according to the executioners themselves, half a *million* "political prisoners" were shot, or 20,000 a month.[29]

To measure these deaths on an historical scale, Solzhenitsyn compared them to the horrors of the Spanish Inquisition, which during the 80-year peak of its existence condemned an average of 10 heretics a month. The difference was this: The Inquisition only forced unbelievers to believe in a world unseen; Socialism demanded that they believe in the very lie that the revolution had condemned them to live.[30]

Occasionally the *New York Times* will offer opinion space to a conservative. William Baude, professor at the University of Chicago Law School, wrote: "Originalism [in the interpretation of the U.S. Constitution] is the closest thing we have to a publicly shared set of

---

[28] Horowitz, p. 79.

[29] Horowitz, pp. 79-80.

[30] Horowitz, p. 80.

legal principles. And it is not time to abandon it."[31] Unfortunately, progressives believe the opposite, that the Constitution is not set in stone, that it is a living document to be constantly interpreted to reflect contemporary public opinion. Let progressives reconvene a Constitutional Convention and they will completely rewrite the Constitution—turn it from a one-page handwritten document into a tightly scripted 254-page European Union Maastricht Treaty, a guide that would allow Congress and the Supreme Court to consider every issue on its merit, without precedent, as if Congress and the Supreme Court had all the time in the world to hear an additional thousand cases a year.[32]

Adhering to "originalism" does not mean absolutely no interpretation, rather, an adherence to precedents, to holdings, what the authors of the Constitution intended. That's why there are nine, not three (originally six), justices on the Supreme Court: to discuss the intent of the law.

Professor Baude concludes: "Originalism has had widespread support for a reason. It has the potential to transcend our moral disagreements. The danger of results-oriented judging is that other people, including future conservative judges, may not share your moral convictions. Originalism is a method of evaluation, not a party platform."[33]

Bill Clinton's Inaugural Address on January 23, 1996, combines both arguments:

- The era of big government is over.

- We know big government does not have all the answers.

---

[31] William Baude, "Why Conservatives Shouldn't Give up on Originalism," *New York Times*, Opinion, July 13, 2020, https://www.nytimes.com/2020/07/09/opinion/supreme-court-originalism-conservatism.html.

[32] In 1937 Franklin Roosevelt tried to add six justices to the Court. Today Roosevelt would have tried for 50—to circumvent "checks and balances" in government, precisely what was preventing him from unilaterally imposing his New Deal on the nation.

[33] Baude, "Why Conservatives Shouldn't Give up on Originalism."

- We know there's not a program for every problem.

- We have to give the American people [a government] that lives within its means.

After that lip service, the address proceeded to outline a long list of things the federal government ought to do. According to Eric Boehm, *Reason* magazine, the above succinct concept of limited government likely would, if expressed today, make a Democrat effectively unelectable—at least on the national stage. "For that matter, the idea that Americans would be able to help themselves best if government got out of the way would place Clinton, circa 1996, outside the emerging mainstream consensus of today's Republican Party. Acknowledging the limits of government power to improve people's lives and worrying about the cost of a large and growing government is, it seems, *so* last century."[34]

Freeland was a welfare state. If a citizen wanted anything from a load of bone meal to a sexual partner some department was ready to offer effective aid. The threat implicit in this enveloping benevolence stifled the concept of rebellion.

—William S. Burroughs, *Naked Lunch*[35]

What is a City?

Ask Jane Jacobs. Ask me. Read this chapter and you will understand why San Francisco should terminate its "liberal" planning

[34] Eric Boehm, "The Era of Small Government Is Over," *Reason*, June 2021, p. 21, https://reason.com/2021/05/08/the-era-of-small-government-is-over/.

[35] William S. Burroughs, *Naked Lunch* (Grove Press, 1959), p. 186.

department. Every thought, every action, of that institution is wrong. The planning department has been ruining the city!

Cities are places of commerce, not places of residence. They are the town marketplace grown large. Tired of commuting, hauling merchandise back and forth from the country, farmers and tradespeople finally just stayed in town. They built residences over their stores and the marketplace became the town center, eventually the city center.

As manufacturers specialized, production increased. Prices of goods dropped, demand rose, the economy grew, standard of living grew: the Industrial Revolution. Commerce is the *sine qua non* of a city.

Only secondarily is a city a place of residence. Nothing should interfere with commerce. Nothing should interfere with manufacturing, transportation, the sale of goods and services. Zoning, taxation, regulation, bike lanes, parks, pedestrian malls— nothing. Put such interference first, and you put the cart before the horse. Put the economy first, and everything falls into place. The invisible hand of the market organizes society better than anything ever done by design. And that is because social, political and economic actions are so inherently interrelated that every act of economic intervention negatively affects all human social and political acts. Don't regulate business!

Why, then, would cities adopt rent control? Not important. Rent control is not the problem; it's a symptom. Supply control is the problem. Rent control, price control, is simply a response to a housing shortage, in San Francisco, of 300,000 units. If San Francisco built those units, the price of its housing would drop in half, immediately. "Affordable housing," no longer an issue.

Building 3,000 to 4,000 units a year, as the city does now, will take 150 years to correct the problem.[36]

More damaging than rent control is the fact that high-cost housing prevents the natural movement of workers from areas of low productivity to areas of high productivity. If San Francisco and the Bay Area continue to restrict the supply of housing, this world center of innovation in technology, artificial intelligence, biological engineering and space flight will shift elsewhere.[37]

City planning goes against the evolution of a city, the ongoing creative equilibrium process that must be allowed to run its course.

Unfortunately, once cities evolve, conservative left-wing forces unite to prevent further natural development. The Left cannot abandon its Utopian vision for a city: a collection of small-town neighborhoods, because it is psychologically incapable of appreciating that in a free economy, protective zoning and the

---

[36] In San Francisco neither landlords nor tenants are complaining about rent control. It's a market distortion that permits both to make off like bandits. Tenants receive virtually free rent for life (no need to save for retirement), and landlords accumulate appreciation of property value far in excess of the loss from submarket rent. [Investment tip: invest in cities with rent control. The rate of return is higher than most other investments.]

Major thoroughfares in San Francisco: Geary Boulevard, Van Ness Avenue, all of South of Market, both sides of Golden Gate Park (Lincoln and Fulton Avenues, our Central Park North and South), plus California Street, Judah, Taraval, and Third Streets, should have ten-story apartment buildings with an express subway line. Residential areas such as the Sunset, Richmond, and Outer Mission districts should be rezoned two to four units per parcel. No other city in the world is comprised of so many single-family homes. Why is Silicon Valley (Santa Clara Valley), the richest agricultural land *in the world*, covered over with asphalt? Because in California, we build out instead of up.

[37] Tyler Cowen, in *The Complacent Class, the Self-defeating Quest for the American Dream* [as stated by Hoover Institute Research Fellow David R. Henderson, reviewer of Cowen's book, in *Regulation* magazine, Spring 2017, p. 51] cites a 2015 National Bureau of Economic Research paper by University of Chicago economist Chang-Tai Hsieh and University of California, Berkeley, economist Enrico Moretti, who have found that lowering regulatory constraints in highly regulated cities such as San Francisco to the level of regulation in median-regulated U.S. cities will expand those high-cost cities' workforces and increase U.S. GDP by 9.5 percent.

restriction of interplay among diverse economic uses cause undesirable homogeneity.

Zoning laws preserve what already exists: In San Francisco, Victorian homes. With absolutely no idea how this inexplicable gift came into existence (like children who inherit wealth without having earned it), city planners are afraid of losing it.

But preservationist zoning does not induce development. New development, the product of creative insight as to what direction a city is headed, is lost when it becomes a public planning vision. Why? Because zoning and planning commissions serve a counter-function: they slow the rate of a city's growth or, worse, create growth where it would never occur on its own. Planners do not know what developers know. Planners, not financially invested, think developers act only from greed—the ultimate in naïveté. Jane Jacobs gives an example of a planning commission at work:

> Consider the Morningside Heights area in New York City. According to planning theory it should not be in trouble at all, for it enjoys a great abundance of parkland, campus, playground and other open spaces. It has plenty of grass. It occupies high and pleasant ground with magnificent river views. It is a famous educational center with splendid institutions—Columbia University, Union Theological Seminary, the Julliard School of Music, and half a dozen others of eminent respectability. It is the beneficiary of good hospitals and churches. It has no industries. Its streets are zoned in the main against "incompatible uses" intruding into the preserves for solidly constructed roomy, middle-and upper-class apartments. Yet by the early 1950s Morningside Heights was becoming a slum so swiftly, the surly kind of slum in which people fear to walk the streets, that the situation posed a crisis for the institutions. They and the planning arms of the city government got together, applied more planning theory, wiped out the most run-down part of the area and built in its stead a middle-income cooperative project complete with shopping center, and a public housing project, all interspersed with air,

light, sunshine and landscaping. This was hailed as a great demonstration in city saving.[38]

After that, Morningside Heights went downhill even faster.

This is not, according to Jacobs, an unfair, irrelevant, or outdated example. In city after city, precisely the wrong areas, in light of planning theory, are decaying. Less noticed but equally significant, in city after city, the wrong areas, in light of planning theory, are refusing to decay.

> Cities are an immense laboratory of trial and error, failure and success, in city building and city design. This is the laboratory in which city planning should have been learning and forming and testing its theories. Instead the practitioners and teachers of this discipline (if such it can be called) have ignored the study of success and failure in real life, have been incurious about the reasons for unexpected success, and are guided instead by principles derived from the behavior and appearance of towns, suburbs, tuberculosis sanatoria, fairs, and imaginary dream cities—from anything but cities themselves.[39]

Morningside Heights is not an outdated example. It's a classic example. In the 1960s, the Redevelopment Agency of San Francisco, a HUD affiliate, destroyed 2,500 Victorian homes, beautiful homes, 883 businesses, 4,729 households, an entire neighborhood, a diverse neighborhood, to build low-income housing.[40] The Western Addition neighborhood was destroyed. A cradle of American jazz (as much as the French Quarter in New Orleans) was destroyed to build cheap and ugly housing.

Another example: As a reaction to urban squalor in late 19th-century London, an attempt was made to create garden cities on its

---

[38] Jane Jacobs, *The Death and Life of Great American Cities,* (New York: Vintage Books, 1961), pp. 5-6.

[39] Jacobs, p. 6.

[40] Leslie Fulbright, "Black Population Deserting San Francisco," *San Francisco Chronicle*, August 10, 2008, https://www.sfgate.com/bayarea/article/Black-population-deserting-S-F-study-says-3274047.php

periphery. The poor would live closer to nature, and industry would be located there. The model conceived by Ebenezer Howard, according to Jane Jacobs, was:

> . . . self-sufficient small towns, really very nice towns if you were docile and had no plans of your own and did not mind spending your life among others with no plans of their own. As in all Utopias, the right to have plans of any significance belonged only to the planners in charge.[41] The Garden City was to be encircled with a belt of agriculture. Industry was to be in its planned preserves; schools, housing and greens in planned living preserves; and in the center were to be commercial, club and cultural places, held in common. The town and green belt, in their totality, were to be permanently controlled by the public authority under which the town was developed, to prevent speculation or supposedly irrational changes in land use and also to do away with temptations to increase its density—in brief, to prevent it from ever becoming a city. The maximum population was to be held to thirty thousand people.[42]

Is the choice, then, between planning and no planning? No. The choice is between private planning and political planning. Even when political planning produces viable projects, still, by definition, the process is un-American. Lobbying government for the privilege of building a project is an aristocratic endeavor only the rich can afford.

City planners further this process. With their collectivist backward-looking vision, like Ebenezer Howard, they think they can design cities better than the market. From inward-looking housing

---

[41] In the 21st century, after years of political failure, for the same reason, reaction to that elitist, controlling mind-set has put Right Wing populists into office, worldwide.

[42] Jacobs, *The Death and Life of Great American Cites,* pp.17-18.
Another example are the apartment buildings that encircle the outskirts of Paris (known as HLM). The thought, according to their architect Le Corbusier was to create high-rise buildings with lots of land around so residents would experience a park setting. Those HLM are an extraordinary gift to the center of Paris. Literally, they moved poor people out of the city, especially poor ethnic minorities. Tourists and citizens of Paris can't believe that Paris is so beautiful, that it has none of the homeless problems that most big city's experience. Collective solutions, however, have another name: fascism.

projects (turning their backs to the street), to the clustered vertical housing surrounded by open space (Le Corbusier in France), to monumental cultural centers such as Lincoln Center in New York and Civic Center in San Francisco, planners have created isolated pockets that would never exist otherwise. *All* are surrounded by seediness. In flawed studies and planning (as to how they really work, how they police themselves, how they exchange ideas, how they operate politically and economically), according to Jacobs, cities have been served up as sacrificial victims.

Great European cities—London and Paris, and great American cities—New York and Chicago, have zoning laws, now, but originally, they evolved naturally, diversely. The desire today to separate residences from the mainstream of ordinary living is unnatural. To emphasize the point, here is my summary, with commentary, of Jacobs' main ideas in *The Death and Life of Great American Cities*:

- Streets and sidewalks are more than a place for circulation. They are where people gather. A city is not a big town. *In a city everyone is a stranger.* Streets and sidewalks must be integral with safety. In a successful city neighborhood, one is not threatened walking on the streets and sidewalks—because *people on the streets lead to safety.* Thinning out the population, as in the suburbs, is not an answer. Los Angeles, one huge suburb, has an enormous crime rate. Few people are on the streets; therefore, few eyes are on the streets. With mixed-use neighborhoods, people have genuine reasons to use a street night and day. People won't look out a window on to an empty street, but they will when there is circulation. All this leads to safety.

- Uniform or beautiful neighborhoods do not make for successful neighborhoods. Beautiful houses and beautiful schools deteriorate the minute a neighborhood changes. Protecting uniform physical qualities ensures nothing. A neighborhood that looks out for itself with some amount of self-governance and interest in its schools will be successful. Neighborhood diversity provides the dynamic for this. A planning commission's ideal of a small town within a city is not how cities work, rather, according to Jacobs, why neighborhoods fail. In a small town, everyone works, plays and shops in the town. Lives constantly crisscross. *This provincialism does not and should not happen in a big city.* That is the point of cities. Mobility leads to diversity in jobs, goods, ideas and culture.

- A planning commission cannot design an entire city. Individuals and neighborhoods acting in their best interest organize cities naturally. Zoning, an administrative tool to ease governance, never encompasses the thousands of variations people normally want for themselves— including the thousands of ideas people do not always articulate but which might find expression if allowed to evolve naturally.

- City planners may appreciate diversity, but the very nature, nay, definition of their job, planning, is to categorize and separate. They create simple models for *their* purposes, bureaucratic ease of processing. Economists, however, abstract models from the whole universe of information. They reconcile real dynamics of nature, supply and demand, by which citizens can solve societal problems. That's what an economy does, what a city does—organizes the individual actions of all citizens, not the actions of their government.

- With their large numbers, cities support diversity—why theaters and art galleries usually do not survive in small towns. More importantly, according to Jacobs, diversity breeds diversity. Support services of diverse activity in close approximation increase diversity, adding to a neighborhood's richness. That's how cities facilitate trade. Zoning not only kills diversity, it kills trade in new and evolving businesses.

According to Jacobs, there are four ingredients for diversity in city streets and districts:

1. City streets and districts should serve more than one function, preferably more than two, and there should be a presence of people on different schedules for different purposes sharing common facilities. This enables the economics of neighborhoods to work. Businesses close, nightlife and culture die when people are not on the streets at all hours.

2. Most blocks should be short, with opportunity to turn corners. Long blocks prevent frequent interchange and tend to concentrate commercial in specific areas (compare New York's Upper West Side with long blocks and commercial jammed onto Columbus Avenue with the Upper East Side's short blocks and commercial interspersed).

3. Buildings should be of various ages. Areas built all at once or with too high a density usually are standardized, leading to uniformity.

4. There should be dense concentrations of people, including residents. Small concentrations, as in towns, lead to cultural and commercial life catered to the habits and prejudices of the majority. Minority opinion finds expression in dense areas. Density, however, need not mean overcrowding—why insisting on too much open space is a mistake; it reduces pedestrian size and neighborhood density. According to Jacobs, most

neighborhoods need more population. City life is promoted by encouraging that which makes a city successful: diversity and large numbers.

Jacobs states that to many people, mixed uses look ugly, cause traffic congestion and invite ruinous uses. People have that impression by observing failures without knowing why they are failures. Those who think mixed use is ugly prefer homogeneity because they see it as order. But homogeneity is monotony, and monotony is ugly. Variance in uniform districts is usually superficial, a pretense at change (such as a façade or roofline) unrelated to a building's function. Genuine diversity is never ugly. If there is traffic congestion, it is because of low density, driving to obtain goods and services instead of walking in one's own area.

If we abandon zoning and let natural market processes organize our cities, will we ruin our cities? *Fear* that this is so is the essence of zoning law. Jane Jacobs' response is worth quoting at length:

> Is it true that city diversity invites ruinous uses? Is permissiveness for all (or almost all) kinds of uses in an area destructive?

> To consider this, we need to consider several different kinds of use—some of which actually are harmful, and some of which are conventionally considered to be harmful but are not.

> One destructive category of uses, of which junk yards are an example, contributes nothing to a district's general convenience, attraction, or concentration of people. In return for nothing, these uses make exorbitant demands upon the land—and upon esthetic tolerance. Used-car lots are in this category. So are buildings which have been abandoned or badly underused.

> Probably everyone (except possibly the owners of such objects) is agreed that this category of uses is blighting.

But it does not follow that junk yards and their like are therefore threats which accompany city diversity. Successful city districts are never dotted with junk yards, but that is not *why* these districts are successful. It is the other way around. They lack junk yards *because* they are successful.

Deadening and space-taking low economic uses like junk yards and used-car lots grow like pigweed in spots which are *already* uncultivated and unsuccessful. They sprout in places that have low concentrations of foot traffic, too little surrounding magnetism, and no high-value competition for the space. Their natural homes are gray areas and the dwindled-off edges of downtowns, where the fires of diversity and vitality burn low. If all controls were lifted from housing-project malls, and these dead, underused places found their natural economic level, junk yards and used-car lots are exactly what would sprout in many of them.

The trouble represented by junk yards goes deeper than the Blight Fighters can plumb. It achieves nothing to cry "Take them away! They shouldn't be there!" The problem is to cultivate an economic environment in the district which makes more vital uses of the land profitable and logical. If this is not done, the land might as well be used for junk yards, which after all have *some* use. Little else is apt to be successful, and this includes public uses, like parks or school yards, which fail catastrophically precisely where the economic environment is too poor for other uses that depend on magnetism and surrounding vitality. The kind of problem symbolized by junk yards, in short, is not solved by fearing diversity, or by suppression, but rather by catalyzing and cultivating a fertile economic environment for diversity. [Not something that government can do.]

A second category of uses is conventionally considered, by planners and zoners, to be harmful, especially if these uses are mingled into residential areas. This category includes bars, theaters, clinics, businesses and manufacturing. It is a category which is not harmful; the arguments that these uses are to be tightly controlled derive from their effects in suburbs and in dull inherently dangerous gray areas, not from their effects in lively city districts.

Thin smatterings of nonresidential uses do little good in gray areas, and can do harm, because gray areas are unequipped to handle strangers—to protect them either, for that matter. But again, this is a problem that arises from too feeble a diversity in the prevailing dullness and darkness.

In lively city districts, where abundant diversity has been catalyzed, these uses do not do harm. They are positively necessary, either for their direct contributions to safety, public contact and cross-use, or because they help support other diversity which has these direct effects.

Work uses suggest another bugaboo: reeking smokestacks and flying ash. Of course reeking smokestacks and flying ash are harmful, but it does not follow that intensive city manufacturing (most of which produces no such nasty by-products) or other work uses must be segregated from dwellings. Indeed, the notion that reek or fumes are to be combated by zoning and land-sorting classifications at all is ridiculous. The air doesn't know about zoning boundaries. Regulations specifically aimed at the smoke or the reek itself are to the point. [This property rights issue will be discussed later.]

Among planners and zoners, the great shibboleth in land use was formerly the glue factory. "Would you want a glue factory in your neighborhood?" was the clincher. Why a glue factory I do not know, except possibly that glue then meant dead horses and old fish, and the reference could be counted upon to make nice people shudder and stop thinking. There used to be a glue factory near us. It was in a small, attractive brick building and was one of the cleanest-looking places on its block.[43]

According to Jacobs, there is one category of use that should be controlled: parking lots, large or heavy trucking depots, gas stations, gigantic outdoor advertising, and enterprises that are harmful not because of their nature, but because in certain streets their *scale is wrong*. All five are profitable enough (unlike junk yards) to afford space in vital diversified areas, but they are street

---

[43] Jacobs, *The Death and Life of Great American Cites,* pp. 230-232.

desolators. They visually disorganize streets. They so dominate that it is hard to counter their sense of order. What's wrong is that they are disproportionally large; they explode the street—make it fly apart such that pedestrians turn around and go back.

————

From an economist's perspective, zoning laws are an attempt to eliminate negative externalities—with a stroke of a pen. But simple solutions to complex problems are an insult to intelligent citizens; they exclude the possibility of variance and negotiation. Politically expedient, they lack subtlety. They are an erosion of property rights. The abnegation of negotiation over uses of land eliminates any possibility of mutual gains from creative voluntary exchange. With strong property rights, neighbors can work out differences by assigning values to them.

They will compare costs and benefits of continuing certain actions. With clearly defined property rights, polluting or selfish behavior (blocking someone's view) involves costs (lawsuits) which can be compared or weighed against benefits. Clearly defined property rights make adjudication possible. According to Paul Heyne, in *The Economic Way of Thinking*, adjudication clarifies property rights, which in turn gives stability to society; people know what to expect.[44] If people do not know what to expect, what others will do, what the "rules of the game" are, chaos results. In this sense, when property rights are clear and enforced, constructive anarchy is possible. That subtlety is lost when zoning laws eliminate non-conforming uses.

Does the convenience of zoning laws outweigh the cost of having to verify and make decisions about the plans of every single neighbor? Do zoning laws provide a benefit that outweighs these verifications and decisions, what economists call transaction costs? On a basic level, to some people the benefit of conformity does outweigh the beauty of diversity. But should society ever realize

---

[44] Paul Heyne, *The Economic Way of Thinking* (MacMillan Publishers, 1987), p. 295.

property rights create value, that value self-protects, incidences where transaction costs occur will be infrequent. Why? Because like-kind uses generally attract each other, and a certain amount of diversity adds value. If transaction costs are infrequent, the total benefit from voluntary exchange far outweighs the cost.

Negative externalities can also be controlled by taxes. In his article entitled "An Economic Analysis of Zoning Laws," part of a Pacific Institute for Public Policy publication entitled *In Resolving the Housing Crisis*, Carl Dahlman states that a role for government could be to restore correct relative prices by using Pigouvian taxes.[45] In other words, activities that confer negative effects on others ought to be taxed so as to confer a subsidy to those affected. That would restore land value. By dealing with specific cases, in economics by thinking marginally, blanket zoning laws are avoided and economic efficiency is achieved. Use of government in this fashion would not be pervasive because land values themselves, a product of market forces, usually eliminate conflicting uses. Dahlman points out that consumers generally factor in externalities before deciding to purchase. Elimination of smog in Los Angeles would not change land use; it would only increase property value. Dahlman feels that zoning laws are really created to stop human migration. With exclusionary zoning, property values rise and broad categories of people are excluded from entering certain neighborhoods or districts.

According to Jacobs, the above argument against exclusive zoning is that it creates borders. The area surrounding an exclusive use has less circulation because it attracts only those using the exclusive use. It creates a vacuum that eats away at the border—why land bordering freeways, railroad tracks, waterfronts, big city university campuses, civic centers, large hospital grounds and large parks are prone to blight.

Instead of creating blight, diversification would unslum slums. According to Jacobs, if a population in an area can be persuaded to stay, society will eliminate transiency, which would

---

[45] Carl. J. Dahlman, "An Economic Analysis of Zoning Laws," in *Resolving the Housing Crisis*, ed. M. Bruce Johnson (Pacific Institute for Public Policy Research, 1982).

eventually attract a middle class. Like the Back of the Yards neighborhood in Chicago, when the middle class stays because they can afford more living space (combining units, for example), a whole process of uncrowding is set in motion. Because they are better able to organize politically, a middle class will demand city services, and because they have bank balances, induce banks to lend in the area.

Planning notions like building new housing and clearing slums do not solve the cause of slums, which is transient populations. It treats the symptoms of their bad effects. Jacobs cites the miracle of Boston's North End in which owners (often tradespeople) bartered services and fixed up their property without borrowing—proving that money is only necessary gradually. As a neighborhood transforms, it comes into its own. Money is not the reason neighborhoods die or do not transform. In the 1960s, according to Jacobs, cataclysmic money (large doses for slum clearance and housing projects) literally destroyed neighborhoods.[46]

Another incorrect planning notion is the idea of reducing automobile traffic. Those who like separating city uses by district usually like reducing automobile traffic. As stated in the opening paragraph, both ideas run counter to what cities are: centers of trade. Cities must accommodate personal transportation needs because trade is a personal matter, not something that exists by formula. People trading goods and services, real things, often in creative ways, require flexibility. Not everyone works nine to five every day at the same location. Attrition of the automobile could be the death of a city. Today's cities are overwhelmed by automobiles because the price to use city streets is too low. At the right price, 50 dollars for parking from nine to five, shoppers and workers would use public transit and creative traders would factor it as a cost of doing business.

---

[46] True also for foreign aid: money is necessary only gradually. Foreign aid, like domestic aid, fails precisely because it comes in massive doses and goes to government agencies rather than to private individuals already in the process of transforming their nation.
  Another example is rent control. It treats the symptom but not the cause of the problem: supply-control.

By allowing cities to grow in size and diversity, because the workplace remains concentrated in a smaller landmass, public transportation becomes practical. If zoning restrictions force populations and businesses to move out, an automobile becomes necessary for work.

Incorrect notions of planning and zoning carry over into incorrect notions of design, namely, that cities *can* be designed. That cities can be works of art, according to Jacobs, is impossible. Art is a rigorous process by an individual artist. Cities evolve spontaneously. They solve problems of trade and communication. They are beyond design. Art is abstraction. Cities, like life itself, are reality. According to Jacobs, city design is taxidermy—it stuffs someone's ideas of harmony into permanency. Creation of beautiful cities, by its very process, must be undemocratic: someone has to set and enforce standards for everyone. Although we are nostalgic for them, natural cities, like American Indian cliff dwellings or coastal towns along the Mediterranean, are a product of limited resources and a structured and conforming society. They do not work in a democracy. In fact, the employment of natural architectural design criteria, once a city has adopted a master plan, becomes impossible. Planners with their small-town communal vision rule out exceptions. San Francisco could never have cliff dwellings on Telegraph Hill or geodesic domes South of Market. San Franciscans have permanently encapsulated 1890s Victorian design, satisfying to the pioneers who made the dangerous crossing of the Great Plains, after which all they wanted was a cheerful little home, but not great architecture. Why, then, is the city's residential construction still a knockoff of that period?[47]

Good architecture or planning reflects and illuminates the functioning of an area. Plans that limit an area with borders or impose uniformity in design kill vitality and limit natural expansion. With respect to salvaging housing projects, Jacobs connects these

---

[47] The mandate to build the Golden Gate Bridge was rammed down the throats of a fiercely objecting planning commission. San Francisco's pyramid building, originally designed twice as large, was also nixed by that commission. You wouldn't want the Eiffel Tower in the middle of town, would you?

ideas. She recommends abandoning limits, especially income limits. *Anyone* should be allowed to move in. That would create the diversity that would make people want to live in projects, the only way they can be saved.

Planners cannot save the projects they approved. A tragedy of the commons (tragedy from collective rather than private ownership), those projects should be turned over to the private sector, perhaps to the occupants themselves. If nations enforce property rights, the market will solve their housing needs. It is what the market does best.

The market is perfectly capable of providing safe construction—without planning department building codes. Norman Karlin, writing in the Pacific Research Institute's publication, *In Resolving the Housing Crisis*, "Zoning and Other Land Use Controls," argues that it should be insurance companies who inspect and guarantee safety.[48] To Karlin, this is no different than pest control companies guaranteeing against pests and dry rot, or title insurance companies guaranteeing against title defects. Building codes exist to ease government monitoring, but with a cost to society: uniformity. Allow diversity, and private parties personally invested and with genuine interest will create economic efficiency. Uniform building codes and zoning serve only to prevent the emergence of scales relative to individual situations. Planners, with nothing at stake, who see everything as overwhelming complexity, do not trust the market. Get rid of them! Why can't private inspection companies rate buildings for safety and design?[49] Why can't safety levels be determined by weighing marginal benefits

---

[48] Norman Karlin, "Zoning and Other Land Use Controls," in *Resolving the Housing Crisis: Government Policy, Decontrol and the Public Interest* (Pacific Research Institute for Public, 1982).

[222] With San Francisco on a fault line, the Department of Building Inspection (DBI) in 2013 ordered all apartment buildings be seismically upgraded, . . . (Continued on next page)

against marginal costs?[50] Ironically, that is how building codes are established in France, a country that loves regulation and central planning: insurance companies write and enforce the codes.[51]

Adapting from methods of analytical reasoning developed in the life sciences, Jacobs concludes *The Death and Life of Great American Cities* by comparing cities to the phenomenon of organized complexity. Unlike simplicity and disorganized complexity, which fall into recognizable patterns of predictability and probability, organized complexity consists of interrelationships that are too difficult to analyze with much certainty. Big cities fall into this category. It is why neighborhoods can be successful in spite of flaws in design and be failures in spite of excellent design. Dynamic cities are beyond design and planning. According to Jacobs, they are a function of processes; they are a catalyst for processes. Cities cannot be ordered like bland suburbs. To do so is to disrespect their essence.

———————

Zoning has eroded property rights in a way the framers of the Constitution could not have envisioned. Why? Because zoning laws are a function of another vision—a social vision of public rather than individual rights. The framers believed citizens had the natural right to their life, liberty and property—but that's all. From a political perspective, they would have seen exclusionary laws as

———————————————

(Continued from previous page) yet allows steel rebar to be inspected by private engineering firms approved by the city. If these firms say the rebar is the correct gauge, placed and connected correctly, concrete may be poured without DBI inspecting the work.

[50] The marginal benefit of a building regulation must outweigh its marginal cost. As environmental regulation considers marginal benefit versus marginal cost, despite "liberal" attempts to prevent this way of thinking, construction regulation should not let the level and cost of seismic upgrade exceed its benefit and push thousands of property owners into bankruptcy (when the damage has been done; those buildings already exist). The solution in the long run is to replace them as they wear out. That's marginal analysis: decisions based on the reality of the moment.

[51] Insurance companies have an incentive to enforce the codes: if things go wrong, *they* pay. Government employees, city planners, unlike developers or insurance companies who have skin in the game, don't pay if things go wrong.

undemocratic. From an economic perspective, as a taking of private property. Economists today would explain this just drives up property values and locks everyone into place. Once nations understand that property rights are a surrogate for zoning laws, they will have also understood that the main purpose of a free economy is to create prices. Important, because except in dictatorships, prices are the only basis from which an economy can be coordinated; the only basis for economic efficiency, for a constantly rising standard of living, for individual liberty.

Another Planning Department

> This week the San Francisco Board of Education voted 6 to 1 to proceed with a plan to rename 44 of the city's currently shuttered schools, wiping away notables like Abraham Lincoln, George Washington, Paul Revere, Robert Louis Stevenson and even Dianne Feinstein, California's senior senator, for various forms of cooperation with white supremacy and patriarchy.[52]

The Mayor, London Breed, had an immediate comment: "What I cannot understand is why the School Board is advancing a plan to have all these schools renamed by April [2021], when there isn't a plan to have our kids back in the classroom [COVID-19]."[53]

More egregious than the name scrubbing is the fact that the board found time to start its revisionism while the city was suing the district for "failing to come up with a reopening plan that meets state requirements."[54]

---

[52] Ross Douthat, "San Francisco Schools, Radicalism and the Pandemic," *New York Times*, January 30, 2021, https://www.nytimes.com/2021/01/30/opinion/san-francisco-school-renaming.html.

[53] Douthat, *New York Times*.

[54] City Attorney Dennis Herrera, with support from Mayor London Breed, sued the San Francisco Unified School District and Board of Education to reopen the schools. (Continued on next page)

So preoccupied with alternative explanations of American history, with multiculturalism, with such goals as removing barriers to equal access (as if after 50 years of busing and focused attention on matters of equality San Francisco's diverse student body really experiences barriers) with such social engineering as mixing students from high and low social backgrounds rather than high and low economic backgrounds (which simply means letting high-performing students in poor neighborhoods enroll in any school they want), or with the politically correct goal of never offending a student's sensibilities (having never read one of the world's great education theorists, Piaget, who said that wasn't necessary, that children's egos are so large, children so self-centered, they recover from just about any scolding), or with the educationally incorrect goal of never giving low grades (accompanied by pressure on principals and teachers never to give parents a reason to complain yet, if they do, never back up the teacher—because, "We're here for the students; because teachers can be replaced but students, our customers, cannot. They have been leaving the district at a rate of 800 a year for the last 50 years: 92,653 in 1970,[55] 52,898 in 2020."[56])

The consequence: teachers lowered standards. The curriculum level in 2000 is exactly one-half what it was in 1965. This author knows: after 12 years a student, K-12, then 40 years a teacher, I know the Board of Education focuses on everything but the issues that underlie education—which is why the board will never address the issues outlined in the next chapter, "Letter to the Board of Education."

(Continued from previous page) The lawsuit is the first of its kind in California and possibly the nation. Jocelyn Gecker, "San Francisco Sues its Own School District to Reopen Classes," Associated Press, February 3, 2021, https://apnews.com/article/san-francisco-sues-own-school-district.

[55] Paul Lorgerie and Jeremy Adam Smith, "San Francisco Schools' Changing Demographics, *San Francisco Private Press*, February 2, 2015, https://www.sfpublicpress.org/san-francisco-schools-changing-demographics/.

[56] Ida Mojadad, "City Schools Losing Students," *San Francisco Examiner*, January 7, 2021, http://sfexaminer.com/news/city-schools-losing-students. (The SFUSD website reports 55,500 students.)

Letter to the Board of Education

Articles about public education miss the following underlying truths:

1. Public education may provide the ability to succeed in life, but that's not the purpose of public education. We have publicly funded schools in this country for one reason: to teach reading, math and history so that students, future citizens, will recognize threats to democracy. Thomas Jefferson created the nation's first public schools because he feared that without an informed citizenry, our new democracy would not survive.

2. To deal with socially and educationally deprived students, systems of classroom management have become the dominant feature of public education. Except that once teachers realize that's what they're actually paid to do, they quit. Since 1970, nationwide, according to the California Commission on Teacher Credentialing and the National Center for Education Statistics (NCES), there have been periods when 50 percent of new teachers leave the profession within three years, 75 percent within five. Those numbers are lower today but, still, in no other sphere do young people enter with such enthusiasm and preparation, then, find their hopes so quickly and thoroughly dashed.

3. All learning is self-learning. Teachers facilitate and motivate learning, but it is students who must do the work.

   School districts paying for small class sizes are wasting their money. The number of students in a class has nothing to do with the number of hours students study.

Statistics do not show that students in small classes learn more than students in large classes. The real reason public schools have small classes is to prevent teachers from quitting.

All learning occurs between the ages of zero and three. Children from socially deprived homes enter kindergarten with a 2,500-to 4,500-word deficit, which increases through grade 12.[57] Since the 1970s, public schools, catering to the socially deprived, have driven away their best students and teachers.

4. To raise test scores (overnight), school districts need do only one thing: bring back their best students and teachers! Unapologetically bring back academic standards, a Eurocentric classical education. It's time for America to reunite behind its common culture: 5th century Athens, 1st century Rome, 18th century Age of

---

[57] Canadian Language and Literary Research Network, Ontario Institute for Studies in Education, University of Toronto, "Handbook of Language and Literary Development: A Roadmap from 0 to 60 Months," Andrew Biemiller, London, Ontario, 2009, http:// theroadmap.ualberta.ca/vocabularies.

> I estimate that by the beginning of kindergarten, children's vocabulary size ranges from 2,300 root word meanings (average for children with low vocabularies) to 4,700 root word meanings (average for children with high vocabularies).

> During the grades from kindergarten to grade two, the difference between children with small and large vocabularies continues to get larger. By the end of grade two, children in the low vocabulary group average 4,000 root word meanings, children in the average vocabulary group know about 6,000 meanings, and children in the large vocabulary group average 8,000 meanings. These large vocabulary differences have developed *before* children have had much of an opportunity to build vocabulary from their own reading. Beginning readers (kindergarten-grade two) mainly read "primer" texts using relatively few words.

Dana Suskind, University of Chicago Medicine, founder of the *Thirty Million Words Initiative,* encourages parents of disadvantaged families to read and relate to their children: to develop the brain, which by age four has heard 30 million fewer words than advantaged children.

Enlightenment, the culture of British and American democracy, individual freedom; in sum, Western civilization.

It's important because without common culture, America will not be able to defend itself from domination by countries that do have a common culture, which is every other country in the world, China, for example.

It's important because America is unique among nations in being founded on a set of ideas and values rather than on a shared "identity." But this inspiration is being obliterated by multiculturalism and identarian politics, both of which go against the credo, *e pluribus unum* ("out of many, one"), as they focus on the injustices rather than the values of the Founding Fathers.

There is an experience gap in our national culture. We no longer have the same appreciation: that America was "conceived in liberty" (Abraham Lincoln), as a refuge from persecution and corruption. Why was the 400-year anniversary of the Pilgrims landing at Plymouth Rock, November 11, 1620, not celebrated in 2020, not even mentioned? It is what Americans have in common: some forebear of their family fled their country to come here, to escape something awful. [African-Americans included. See Chapter 2, "400 years."] And then, the Pilgrims and Indians worked together (at first). Unfortunately, news of the success of the Pilgrims spread throughout England and rogue individuals followed who exploited the situation—offering guns and alcohol to the Indians, absolutely undoing the original efforts of the Pilgrims. Read *Of Plymouth Plantation: The Journal of William Bradford*, the authoritative account of the history and arrival of the Pilgrims and their life at Plymouth Colony from 1620 to 1660.

There is an experience gap because Americans today take too much for granted and are unaware of the nation's roots: the culture of British and American democracy—where such things as due process, *habeas corpus*, common law built over centuries, civil rights to life, liberty and property and limited government, historically, has been guaranteed *only* in Britain and America.

5. Public Schools do not offer a report card that reflects a student's level of achievement:

Subject	Grade level	Grade
English	6	C-
Math	4	B
PE	11	B+[58]

Students not prepared to work at grade level should be given a voucher to attend private school. Private schools should be for troubled students, public schools for good students.

And only students at grade level should take state or national tests—and only in the fourth, eighth and twelfth grades. Not only will this raise California test scores, but it will stop schools from wasting so much time, *every year*, preparing for tests, worse, teaching to the test! California's ranking will jump from 42nd in the nation [*Education Week*, 2017] to second or third.

6. The problems of American public education are not due to a lack of funding. They are due to *too much funding*. We spend more than is optimal, more than any other

---

[58] The student deserved an A, but half the time came to class in street clothes. Do professional athletes show up without a uniform?

nation. From 1970 to 2000, nationwide, spending per pupil doubled, yet test scores dropped 25 percent. For every $1,000 of increased spending, SAT scores dropped ten points. See graphs next page. From 2000 to 2019, test scores remained flat. See National Center for Education Statistics, U.S. Department of Education.

This is because additional money for education is spent on additional programs—multicultural awareness, arts, sciences, field trips—all of which take time away from basic instruction. KIPP public charter schools are an example of how that additional funding should be used. KIPP schools lengthen their school day by two or three hours plus teach on Saturday. Most public schools do the opposite. To accommodate additional programs, they shorten basic instruction time, achieving what in economics is termed "diminished marginal utility of the funds."

To double test scores, cut spending in half.

7. Test scores are a fraud on the public. Raising a school district's test scores to 50, the national average, is meaningless. If we were a nation of geniuses, 50 would be the national average. A nation of morons, 50 would be the national average. With 36 percent of fourth and eighth grade public school students "proficient" in reading, 40 percent in math, *that* is the national average, 50: failure. See National Center for Education Statistics, U.S. Department of Education, 2015.
    Superintendents know but never acknowledge this. Pretending to be CEOs with pay contingent upon the rise of their company's stock, superintendents want their compensation to be contingent upon the rise of their district's test scores—a meaningless achievement.

This graph shows plummeting test scores:

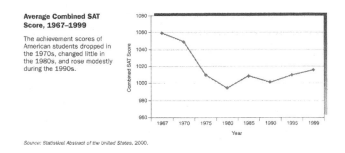

Average Combined SAT Score, 1967–1999

The achievement scores of American students dropped in the 1970s, changed little in the 1980s, and rose modestly during the 1990s.

Source: Statistical Abstract of the United States, 2000.

This graph shows ever-increasing funds for education:

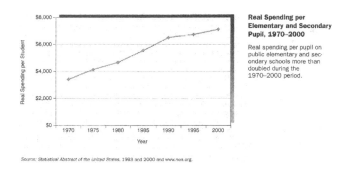

Real Spending per Elementary and Secondary Pupil, 1970–2000

Real spending per pupil on public elementary and secondary schools more than doubled during the 1970–2000 period.

Source: Statistical Abstract of the United States, 1993 and 2000 and www.nea.org.

59

And finally, you, the Board of Education, should listen to what liberals in San Francisco and across the nation said (online) in response to the *New York Times* article cited at the beginning of this chapter—about your attempt to erase the names of schools that reflect the history of this nation:

---

59 James D. Gwartney, *Microeconomics: Private and Public Choice*, 10th Edition (Thomson South-Western, 2003), p. 468. The author also notes there that in 2000,the United States spent $7,764 per secondary pupil, 38 percent *above* the OECD average, but that eighth-grade mathematics achievement scores in 2001 were 3.3 percent lower than the OECD average (OECD, "Education at a Glance," 2001, https://www.oecd.org/education/skills-beyond-school/educationataglance2001-home.htm.)

I would understand the hyper focus on this issue if San Francisco had high-functioning schools. But it doesn't. There are only a handful that are competitive with public schools in other states. Many parents who understand this, [who] care about their children's actually "learning," and can afford it, move away or send them to private schools. The public schools are more focused on wallpapering over disparities rather than educating diverse populations to be competitive in the US workforce. Administrators call rigorous education "perfectionist culture," and explain that "children don't need to learn how to spell when they're going to use spell check." A friend of mine (who is white) said that his daughter came home from a SF public middle school one day, crying. She asked him, "Did white people do anything good?" True stories. These educators/ philistines prefer to focus on political correctness rather than supporting the students. Mayor Breed knows this. The teacher's union supports all this political correctness. It's really difficult to teach students who are underprepared and failing. And probably don't speak or read and write so well. So, refocus on what is easy and give yourself a raise.

—Mariabraun, San Francisco

Sorry Ross, you don't understand San Francisco, especially the school board. It has always been a stepping stone to either a run for supervisor or assembly. And it has had more than its share of members who don't fully think things through when it comes to political correctness and cancel culture.

—Steve Ziman, San Rafael

My husband and I are both progressive liberals. When we heard about this decision by the SF school board, we looked at each other, shook our heads and said,
"This is why America hates us."

—Andrea, Florida

148

I also think it is a bit disingenuous to place ourselves above the icons of the past, as though we could never make the same errors of judgment however genuinely poor —because that precludes learning from them ourselves, and recognizing that Right or Left we all contain the same seeds of both good and evil within us.

—Carla, NYC

This silliness by the "oh so sensitive" Left is exactly the type of thing that is fertilizer to continue to grow the far Right. This isn't an action based on academics and scholarship. It is a ridiculous example of false "wokeness" that stains liberalism with its petty anti-intellectualism.

—Wiff, California

Forty Years a Teacher

At age 24, at the commencement of my teaching career, coincident with the appearance of multiculturalism, postmodernism (the idea that Western civilization is just one approach), I understood that the career before me would be in the service of a system in decline. I could have withdrawn and chosen not to serve; instead, I followed through and paid the price. At times badly treated, as a libertarian among progressives, I thought I could work independently. Like the industrialists in *Atlas Shrugged*, my mistake, then, was to work within the system. Like those industrialists, I, too, did not recognize that the integrity of my own work would be used against me; for example, while I was made to feel unwelcome, my successful concerts were used to showcase how well my schools "appeared" to be doing.

By the end of my career, the hypocrisy had completely backfired. On the day of my Spring Concert (at an elementary school where I had a huge instrumental and choral program), just before going on stage, the principal approached me and said, "I can see that you have more children on stage than in the audience, that your curriculum is truly multicultural, that the level of performance at this school has never been higher, but don't come back next year. You don't belong. You're not one of us."

A year later, I took students from one school to another to create a combined orchestra. The understanding was that on the day of the performance, the number of students who would be allowed to go—fifth-graders first, then fourth, then third—would depend upon how many parent drivers showed up (not simply volunteered). I told the only third-grader that she would probably not go, but promised to take her next year. Sure enough, we were short a driver. And sure enough, her Latina mother complained to the Latina principal, who, then, said, "Watch this!" and made a phone call to central office. After 15 years at that school but only one for the new principal, she had this Caucasian author transferred to another school. Why she couldn't drive the student herself or give the mother and daughter bus fare to travel ten blocks is not clear. What is clear is that mother, child and principal were "entitled."

The final straw was the state of California's latest "Directive": All Teachers Must Enroll in a Two-Year Course in Multicultural Awareness. After 40 years of intensive multicultural teacher training at great public expense, education bureaucrats at the state capital, anxious to show that they had something new to offer (i.e., save their jobs), decided that Eurocentrism and teacher insensitivity to the cultural needs of minorities was the problem; that California teachers, though ranked among the nation's best, with master's degrees in education from the University of California and Stanford, were to blame for the drop in ranking of California's public schools from first in the nation in the 1960s to near last from the year 2000 on.

I asked for an exemption. I indicated that I understood the problems of non-native speakers, having been a foreign student myself, that I had a foreign language teaching credential, spoke four languages and was genuinely appreciative of all cultures, having performed professionally with musicians of all ethnic backgrounds as well as having taught inner-city public schools for 40 years. Denied the exemption, I was told, "If we do this for you, others will ask for it (plus we know older teachers like you will refuse, and we can replace them with younger teachers at half the salary)."

In my last year, I showed up for work in September, following detailed instructions as to where to report for the first days of teacher meetings. After several hours, I noticed my name was not on the sign-in roster. Someone suggested, "You'd better run down to Human Resources and resign—immediately. You are about to lose your health insurance and maybe your pension." My gamble, that the district would not really enforce its absurd directive, didn't pay off.

Perhaps what didn't pay off was 40 years of political incorrectness, for example, returning from summer break and making remarks such as, "Where is Ms. Jones, the school's best teacher? And, "Where's Suzy, my best trumpet player? Did they move to an artist colony?" Not appreciated. Both had withdrawn their attendance. Suzy transferred to a private school; Ms. Jones quit.

For the last 30 years, according to the California Commission on Teacher Credentialing, 50 percent of new (meaning young, bright, enthusiastic, well-trained) teachers quit within three years; 75 percent within five years. Although less so today, the statistic speaks for itself. The less obvious statistic is that over a 30-year period, when one teacher per year and one student per year leave, no one is left—except those at the bottom; no mystery, then, that California test scores are at the bottom.[60]

How did that happen? One reason is that California, conforming to a nationwide vogue, forces teachers to "teach to the test," the most unZen, unWaldorf, unprofessional approach possible. This *diktat* only serves to push out the most creative students and teachers, even administrators, to satisfy that vague "community" need for equality of outcome (rather than individual achievement).

---

[60] As a product of San Francisco public schools and proud of my state, I sent $250,000 to the Mississippi Department of Education with the provision it be used to raise test scores such that they surpass California. (Continued on next page)

Couple it with equality of input, paying the worst teachers the same as the best, giving the worst students the same attention as the best, and *voilà*, you have a major reason for the scholastic results of political correctness.

Transfer that politicalized formula to private industry and you have the story of *Atlas Shrugged*, in which the private sector is rewarded (with state assistance) for failure rather than ability, in which objective standards of excellence are replaced with relative standards, in which the rights of industries in need take precedence.

The solution for the public schools is the solution and principal action in *Atlas Shrugged*: an *owner's* strike. "Workers of the world, *you* try running an industry!" "Parents of the world, *you* try teaching in a public school!"

Socialists assume that society can change just one thing, ownership of the means of production, or ownership of the schools, and that nothing else will change: that the industrialists whose property you confiscated will stick around to help operate their former factories, that teachers well prepared to teach American and European history, culture, and democracy will stick around to coach their multicultural replacements.

————

With one finger, I tapped two students on the wrist to get them to stop talking. The parents of these students asked for a full hearing before the principal to resolve the incident. Their dysfunctional home life caused them to continually act up to get attention, yet those two students never missed my class. I allowed them to remain

————

(Continued from previous page) Why? Because that would make California eligible for the world contest for worst-performing public schools, held inappropriately on the island of Guam, where shoeless children sitting on wooden benches, writing on chalkboards, throwing coconuts at each other scored 50 points higher on the same fourth-grade math test taken by students in California. (Guam, a U.S. protectorate, is subject to U.S. education requirements—why citizens of Guam are thankful not to be a protectorate of Japan or China where education requirements are considerably more rigorous.) The check was sent back.

for the very reason that for my entire teaching career, I taught their age level— namely, that when I was their age, ten, I was them.

Running scared, the principal said to me, "I will script the entire meeting and tell you exactly what to say. The last thing I want is the Board of Education coming here to question me about following their directives."

———————

Music students throughout the district were invited to Lowell High School for a lecture presentation by Dizzy Gillespie. The rules of invitation were strict: music students who did not qualify for federal supplementary funding from the Elementary Secondary Education Act (ESEA) could not attend. In the school where I taught, most students qualified, but none of my music students did. Their parents cared for them just enough for them not to be classified as socially and economically deprived.

The auditorium at Lowell High School that day was filled— with low-achieving restless students. Unaware, Mr. Gillespie spoke to them about 1960s Black pride and political activism, telling the students that they were the Black community's next generation of leaders.[61] He encouraged them to continue their studies. Mr. Gillespie knew that ESEA was funding his presentation, but he had no idea what that really meant—which is that he was wasting his time, taxpayer's money, the time of the 50 teachers who brought the students, the time of the students themselves who would have been better off staying in the classroom. It was all very disturbing.

———————

At close range, a student burped in my face. I touched the student on the cheek to let him know that was not acceptable. I told the

———————

[61] Not so different from conversation in the teachers' lunchroom: "I don't see why we have so many white teachers and downtown personnel at this school. We're perfectly capable of running our own schools." I reminded them of *Brown v. Board of Education*.

principal. After ten years of volunteer teaching at her school, she said, "Walk out, NOW. Do not come back."

One hundred students were waiting to rehearse the Spring Concert (chorus and recorders) plus 15 intermediate recorders expecting to rehearse their graduation: irrelevant. The student who burped in my face was known to the principal to be perpetually out of control: irrelevant. I hadn't hit the student—I just touched him: irrelevant. I pleaded with the principal to reconsider. Via emails I told her I loved that teaching job and suggested that the student and I simply apologize to each other. "Absolutely not!"

I replied that if her decision was based on district policy (of which I wasn't aware), I understood. If based solely on her intolerance of a teacher ever touching a student, I didn't understand. Had this principal, who greeted me every morning with, "We all love you, Mr. Parker," been secretly waiting for this moment? Under the circumstances, tossing out an experienced and dedicated teacher does not demonstrate leadership. Plus, I can never teach again.[62]

———————

Ludwig Wittgenstein, arguably the greatest philosopher of the 20th century, was deeply sincere and unsparingly self-critical. He trained to be an elementary school teacher and taught in Austria from 1920 to 1926. Prone to confession, he admitted that he had hit a schoolgirl for misbehaving. But upon interrogation by the headmaster, Wittgenstein, in the pupil's presence, denied the accusation.[63]

I should never have reported the incident, namely, because it's not possible to be a sensitive, educated and disciplined human being, over a long period of time of teaching students, many of whom are poorly raised, indifferent and obnoxious, and never once

———————

[62] The captain of a ship at sea at war cannot bend the rules because in a particular circumstance they are unfair. –Herman Melville, *Billy Budd*. Are California public schools a ship at sea at war?

[63] Jonathan Beale, "Wittgenstein Confession," *New York Times*, September 21, 2018, https://www.nytimes.com/2018/09/18/opinion/wittgensteins-confession-philosophy.html

give a remonstrative tap. Of course, Wittgenstein lied—though it affected his conscience for years afterward.

These examples illustrate what it means for a nation to have politicized its public schools. Compensating for past discrimination, blaming a Eurocentric curriculum for poor Black and Latin test scores (as if those students could not possibly relate to Western civilization, i.e., to the idea of individual freedom), public education has "entitled" parents and students to special treatment—exactly what Frederick Douglass and Martin Luther King Jr. both warned against. All that Douglass and King asked for was that this nation enforce its civil rights laws *equally*.

As with the politicized economic environment in *Atlas Shrugged*, for today's politicized educational environment, Ayn Rand would have suggested that teachers and administrators withdraw their services. An alternative, of course, would be for teachers and administrators to stick together.

August 15, 2019

Dear Ray,[64]

Thank you for a very perceptive response to "40 Years a Teacher." You exposed a real gap in my understanding of bureaucracy.

It never occurred to me to get representation from the teacher's union or that the public schools might owe me due process before sending me from one school to another or, in the end, telling me to get lost. I at least deserved a hearing.

I taught at San Francisco inner-city public schools for 40 years, in the Mission, Bayview, Visitacion Valley and Oceanview, because I love and respect the students and parents there. Teaching kept me down to earth—so down, I forgot that I have rights too. Amazing. Yes, I do have seniority and 40 years of evaluations, all of which were "excellent." One principal said, "Your teaching is a little unorthodox, but the students are so mesmerized by your presence that one can hear a pin drop. Keep it up, Mr. Parker."

With the last firing, half the faculty (I was told) went to the principal and said, "Hey, you can't just throw out one of the school's best teachers!" Pretty nice, huh?

I probably could sue the school district, but as a volunteer for the last ten years (50 years a teacher total), the only damage done is to my reputation. Should I make a scandal, get the newspapers involved, make the Board of Education read my "40 years"?

Again, Ray, thank you.

Sincerely,

David

---

[64] Dr. Ray Rivera, Director of Mission Mental Health Outreach Center, run by the city of San Francisco.

Woke Liberalism

"Some think there is no such thing as knowledge, since we must first know the ultimates. Others think that there is knowledge, but that all things are demonstratable. Neither view is true or necessary." Or, Aristotle continues, "Can the posterior be known through the prior if there are no first or ultimate points?" For Aristotle, "the infinite cannot be exhausted." "Even if there are end points, a start and a terminus, they are unknowable because they cannot be demonstrated."[65]

These thoughts describe postmodernism, but postmodernism is *not* Aristotle. Truth to Aristotle is *not* a supposition. America's understanding of freedom is *not* arbitrary. All cultures are *not* equal. The ideas of America's identarian subculture are not all of equal importance. The ideas of the Founding Fathers are not hypothesis. The syllogism, "Prosperity is a function of freedom; freedom a function of no constraint; therefore, prosperity a function of no constraint," is not wordplay. That syllogism underlies the U.S. Constitution, a short set of rules for governing a nation that establish maximum individual freedom and maximum government restraint.

The hypothesis that prosperity is a function of no constraint on the individual is not difficult to disprove. Identarian postmodernists simply declare that the measure of prosperity is different for every culture—why, for example, through the internal personal tranquility of Confucianism, without social, political and economic freedom, the Chinese consider themselves prosperous; or through closeness to nature without any notion of social, political or economic freedom, American Indians consider prosperity a nonissue. Indifferent to political freedom, the Chinese ask only to be allowed to make a little money and be with their family, i.e., to keep some of what they produce for trade, knowing that's how wealth is acquired, how standard of living is increased: "Communism with Chinese characteristics." Not demanding social or political freedom, demanding only a little economic freedom, not even the right to own

---

[65] Aristotle, *The Philosophy of Aristotle*, Selections from "Posterior Analytics, Book I," trans. J. L. Creed and A. E. Wardman (Mentor Books, 1963), pp. 163-164.

property (the only protection citizens have against the state), the Chinese agree with Lao Tzu and Machiavelli: "Give the masses a little economic freedom and they will be so grateful *they* will take care of all of society's needs." The president of China need not govern with an iron hand; his masses are not seeking the freedoms achieved by the American Revolution. Eastern culture is not western culture.

Unfortunately, so, too, are Americans no longer demanding such freedom. Influenced by European socialism, Americans today no longer demand complete economic freedom or absolute free speech. Secure in their multiculturalism, in their censorship of offending speech, in their regulation of the economy, Americans today are not aware of the freedoms they have lost, the trade-offs they have made, the tyranny they are creating.

A survey conducted by the Gallup organization and the Knight Foundation finds that 61 percent of students believe their campus climate prevents students from expressing their views for fear of offending others. Heterodox Academy created and validated Its Campus Expression Survey, which found that rates of self-censorship are highest among students who do not conform to the politically progressive views of their peers. A survey conducted by the Foundation for Individual Rights in Education (FIRE) finds the same pattern.[66]

When this happens, unpopular arguments are disallowed or crowded out. In groups that feel they have the moral high ground, heretics get cast out, and a single unchallenged ideology prevails. Without any formal rules, censorship takes place.

Alexis de Tocqueville praised associational life in America. He also recognized the dark side and how members of a majority with a dominant point of view can exercise great power to intimidate, to curtail liberties, to curtail free speech. At a social party

---

[66] Emily Chamlee-Wright, CEO of The Institute for Humane Studies, George Mason University, "Self-Censorship and Associational Life in the Liberal Academy, December 2, 2019, https://www.researchgate.net/journal/Society-/publication/Self-Censorship_and_Associational_Life_in_the_Liberal_Academy/.pdf.

of liberal progressives, a woman pulled out a card she always kept in her purse, and read it aloud:

> the loneliness of a Black among whites;
> the loneliness of a Jew among gentiles;
> the loneliness of a gay among straights.

I added,

> the loneliness of a conservative among liberals.

Dead silence. Not on their radar. Conservative, bad; liberal, good. *That* is in their scope.

On election day 2020, while Donald Trump was still holding his own, one of those at that same party, and hosting a podcast to fellow artists, declared (on Zoom), "We don't know who these people are."

Do progressives really believe that half the nation are "deplorables?" If they don't pay attention, in 2024, they may again be asking, "What happened?"

If identarian subcultures focus exclusively on rights that are of interest only to them, this nation's primary rights will fall into second position. That *is* the case today in America's universities and public schools where for the last 40 years, having focused exclusively on the rights and needs of the bottom quartile, on raising their test scores rather than guaranteeing high educational and behavioral standards for all students, multiculturalists have driven America's curricula into second position. It's why today's public schools, like public housing and public prisons, are an institution of the bottom quartile.

"Without the ability to reason, man will learn nothing at all or he will learn what he already knows."[67]

True in the arts and sciences, in dialectical arguments, in deductive reasoning, true in politics. But according to Aristotle, as long as we agree on what the terms mean, that a triangle has three connected sides, that interior angles add up to 180 degrees, we *can* derive true principles; we *can* take a known truth and derive from it a nonarbitrary universal.[68]

Except in science and math, pure reasoning is neglected in American schools. Worse, students are taught that truth is relative, that every culture has its own truth, that truth is political. *That* is what allows today's college students to insist that college subject matter conform to their already-formed philosophies.

Why do professors not stand up to this? Because they agree? Are afraid? Students should not be asked to defend opinions before having a serious grounding in logic and the fundamental ideas of Western civilization. In the West, for example, the purpose of public education is to teach students that the rights of the individual precede those of the state, that the West is prosperous precisely because freedom leads to opportunity. Thomas Jefferson inaugurated the nation's first public schools so that students would learn history and mathematics so that as adult citizens, they will immediately recognize threats to democracy.[69] If students don't hear the arguments, they won't recognize the threats, which is why today they do not recognize their own postmodernism (their belief that truth is relative) is a threat. Sorry, there is no alternative to Western civilization. Western civilization is not one among many. Western civilization is an evolutionary step forward for mankind. Western

---

[67] Aristotle, *The Philosophy of Aristotle,* pp. 163-4.

[68] A major theme in Ayn Rand's *Atlas Shrugged* is Aristotle's dictum that if A = A, society cannot arbitrarily declare, whenever it wants to, that B = A. If A means "to each according to his ability," A does not also mean "from each accord to his ability," let alone "to each according to his needs." In other words, a nation with a free economy must not control that economy; a nation with a good constitution must not constrain that constitution by changing the meaning of its words.

[69] In America, the purpose of public education is not to provide students an equal opportunity to succeed in life. *That* opportunity is provided by freedom.

civilization is a pinnacle from which a step in any direction is a step down, away from individual freedom, back to aristocracy, to elite leadership, to community and government control. Why today's liberals are today's reactionaries, today's conservatives, today's radicals.

Before criticizing, identarians should ask themselves what would they have done. Are there examples in their lives where they did the right thing and then paid the price: stood up for what they believe and lost their friends or career? If not, they have no right to criticize what others did 200 or 2,000 years ago. Do they understand the pressure those leaders were under? Are they certain that in any of those circumstances they would have risen to the occasion?

Thomas Jefferson inherited Monticello from his father, an incompetent business person who had mortgaged the entire estate. Had he freed his slaves, young Jefferson, a genius studying law, botany (making discoveries), history, philosophy and architecture, would have pitched himself into poverty. His mind, his remarkable library thrown to the winds.[70] Were you he, what would you have done?

Settlers, pioneers moving west, fleeing persecution, poverty, war, pillage and rape in Europe, found themselves surrounded by 200 million buffalo (not 200 thousand), 10 thousand wolves (their homes encircled, wolves howling, not moving), picked off (killed) in their homes by Indians, their food and tools stolen, their hand-hewn homes burned to the ground, out of frustration, got rid of the buffalo, the wolves, the Indians. You would have acted differently? With no fences anywhere, you would have understood you were trespassing?

Joseph Conrad recounts in *Heart of Darkness* piloting a decrepit steamer up the Congo River into the jungle, while being attacked by African tribes along the shore jumping up and down, shooting hundreds of arrows at once, looked into their eyes and felt their humanity. Then, remembering he had to pilot the boat, he disregarded his crazy passengers who got out their shotguns and

---

[70] Jefferson didn't free his slaves, but he did stand up to the British. A handful of American patriots, without an army, stood up to the largest army and navy in Europe and yelled, "You know where we live; come on, burn it down!" You would have done that?

started firing indiscriminately. He had neither the time nor energy for a more creative solution. What would you have done?

The point: discriminated minorities must not hide behind discrimination to explain their failings. The majority has its own problems: Holocaust survivors, war refugees, survivors of ethnic cleansing, survivors of famine, of communism. In the U.S., the opportunity for success far outweighs limitations from discrimination. That is why minorities continue to arrive, why those here stay. Once they realize the majority cannot solve their problems, no matter how guilty the majority are made to feel, minorities will succeed. Reparations? It won't happen. Encircled by white wolves, minorities must push them aside or go around.

> Both my mother and my grandmother grew up in a very traditional South Indian culture, which was hugely misogynistic, but they both, in their own way, found a path for themselves to be productive and useful. They didn't let the beliefs that others held about what women are capable of doing or not doing hold them back. It's not that they didn't understand the limitations that were placed on them by the culture they were living in, but they just went around it or under it.
>
> I learned very quickly the most important lesson any person can learn: You cannot control the world in which you live. You can only control your reaction.
>
> —Padma Lakshmi, cookbook author,
> host and executive producer of
> *Top Chef and Taste the Nation*[71]

Jeane Kirkpatrick, U.S. Ambassador to the UN, was booed off stage at a Boalt Hall lecture at UC Berkeley in 1983.

---

[71] Jennifer Harlan and Alisha Haridasani Gupta, "Eleven Female Voices, From Age 3 to 110, on Why the Vote Matters," *New York Times*, August 26, 2020, https://www.nytimes.com/2020/08/26/us/voting-meaning-women-suffrage.html.

The dean stood up and said, "You children should be ashamed of yourselves."

Kirkpatrick said, "I have not seen a group so interested in denying free speech and discussion."

A student said, "I think it was right. The purpose was to show that people are angry. We've got to look at what is going on in Central America."

The vice-chancellor said, "We have to have some way to deal with those who do not want the university to be a marketplace of ideas, who want to oppress anything they do not want to hear."[72]

None of those adults would have said today what they said then. First, conservative speakers are no longer even invited on campus. Second, those who still advocate that students be exposed to conflicting opinions have learned to self-censor—such as certain professors at UC Berkeley, who fearful of losing their jobs during the McCarthy era in the 1950s, not only kept their mouths shut, but caved in to swearing before congressional hearings of the House Un-American Activities Committee, "I am not a communist!" Today those professors would swear, "I am not a conservative!"[73]

Today, progressive students and faculty control the nation's universities and public schools. They control what they fear: democracy. They don't want to hear everyone's opinion. They want a haven, "safe spaces," from ideas they don't like, ideas they would struggle to understand, for example, that life is unfair, that there is an element of caste in all societies, even in pluralist, ethnically diverse societies. Because it is always self-interest that pushes people (including themselves) to maintain their ranking, their privileges. It is how species survive.

---

[72] Wallace Turner, "Berkeley Divided by a New Dispute over Freedom of Speech," *New York Times*, March 7, 1983, https://www.nytimes.com/1983/03/07/us/berkeley-divided-by-a-new-dispute-over-freedom-of-speech.html.

[73] 1.5 percent of college faculties in the U.S. admit today they are conservative. Conservative professors have been thoroughly intimidated, politically and physically, into self-censorship. David Brooks, "The Future of Nonconformity," *New York Times*, July 24, 2020, https://www.nytimes.com/2020/07/23/opinion/substack-newsletters-writers.html.

> That every will must consider every other will its equal—
> would be a principle *hostile to life*, an agent of the
> dissolution and destruction of man, an attempt to
> assassinate the future of man, a sign of weariness, a secret
> path to nothingness.

—Nietzsche[74]

San Francisco Taxes

Want to start a bakery in San Francisco? You might think that all you need is an oven and a refrigerator. But this liberal city sees you as a capitalist and wants one percent of the value of all your inventory, fixtures, construction costs—everything you spent to get started—*every year* until you close. It's called the Unsecured Business Property Tax. The city needs the money to pay for basic services whose tax revenue has been diverted to special projects the city is famous for: "solving" the homeless problem, generous health insurance and pensions for city employees.[75]

Why is it okay to tax small business? Why are we attacking young people? They save their money, open a business, purchase equipment, then, whether they make a sale or not, the city taxes them. Then adds a payroll tax. With most citizens in this nation working in small business,[76] why does the city disincentivize employers from hiring more workers? Why does San Francisco force

---

[74] Friedrich Nietzsche, *Genealogy of Morals*, trans. Walter Kaufmann (Vintage Books, 1989), p. 76.

[75] The top employer in San Francisco is city government, 6.7 percent of the workforce. "City and County of San Francisco, California Comprehensive Annual Financial Report [2020] for the Year ended June 30, 2019" (PDF) p.243. Civil Service medical benefits include surgery to undergo gender change, plus psychological counseling for job and non-job-related issues, to reverse anti-LGBTQ prejudices, for example.

[76] Over 99 percent of America's 28.7 million firms are small businesses (and account for approximately 45 percent of the nation's GDP). Research: JP Morgan Chase & Co., "Economic Activity," 2021, *https://www.jpmorganchase.com/institute/research/small-business/small-business-dashboard/economic-activity*.

its employers to pay a minimum wage 50 percent above the national minimum wage, plus health insurance—all of which to an employer is a tax to be passed on to the consumer as a price increase for the goods and services they produce, as if that price increase will have no effect on sales, no effect on those companies' ability to remain competitive?

Equally perverse: The city restricts zoning so that almost no new housing is built (3,000 to 4,000 units a year doesn't cut it when 300,000 are needed) then compensates its workforce by enacting rent control. What's next, sales control?

Why is the city mingling in the economy—pushing citizens into two families per household, into sharing automobiles?

———

When young people are saving to buy a first home, why do we force them to save also for retirement, contribute 7½ percent of what they earn to Social Security, plus force their employers to contribute 7½ percent, an additional deduction from their wages? That 15 percent belongs in an employee's savings account earmarked for a down payment on a home. At age 30, *then*, employees can contribute to Social Security (or contribute earlier but have the right to pull out what they need for their down payment). Where in the Constitution does it say government can force citizens to contribute 15 percent of their earnings to a retirement plan, 15 percent to health insurance (the Affordable Care Act, where if you don't purchase health insurance, you are fined), plus 25 to 40 percent in income taxes— precisely what the French (and American docu-satire filmmaker Michael Moore) advocate, a 70 percent tax rate. Is that what it means to live in a free country? With President Biden's American Family Plan, will citizens now have to make an additional contribution to finance a $600 a week universal basic income?

———

Let's attack young people!

In San Francisco, when they leave home and wish to rent their first apartment, let's charge them two or three times what the apartment is worth. Someone has to compensate landlords for their rent-controlled tenants who pay two to three times less than the apartment is worth. And should a young person be provident enough to purchase their first home, he or she faces a property tax five to ten times higher than any neighbor who bought the identical home 30 years ago. California's Prop. 13 property tax on a $100,000 home purchased 30 years ago is $1,100 a year. On that same $1 million home today, $11,000 a year.

Consider Reno, Nevada. It thrives today because its economy is varied (for the first time). Entrepreneurial start-ups, health care and technology-based industry, all are moving there as a market response to "liberal" California, where industry would normally locate, except that in 2021, California has a flat corporate tax rate of 8.84 percent and a personal income tax rate of 13.3 percent. Nevada's corporate tax rate is zero; its personal income tax rate is zero.

Previously, Reno had only one economic base—gambling and entertainment—because it could offer gambling, illegal elsewhere. Today, it offers tax avoidance. Not illegal, but a risky strategy.

Why? Because if California allowed Indians to open casinos (which California did in 2000 and it hit Reno's gambling monopoly hard), what will happen if California lowers its business taxes? Reno's gamble is that California will never lower them enough to make a difference.

Still, Reno, like San Francisco, is for professional investors only. Tesla and Apple are in Reno, but they know what they're doing. They don't care about the economy of Reno—Reno is a branch office. Apple made the same decision when it moved its headquarters to Ireland. Apple doesn't care about the economy of Ireland—it wants the tax advantages. Should Ireland's tax laws change, Apple will move elsewhere. In early 2018, about 90 percent of Apple's total cash on hand, $252 billion, was held on the island of Jersey in the English Channel.[77] In other words, if Reno is at risk of becoming a ghost town, so, too, is San Francisco. Taxation, government regulation of the economy—there is no restraint of trade without a negative consequence. The benefit never outweighs the cost.

---

[77] Josh Hoxie, "Commentary: Apple Avoided $40 Billion in Taxes. Now It Wants a Gold Star?," *Fortune*, January 18, 2018, www.fortune.com/2018/01/18/apple-bonuses-money-us-350-billion-taxes-trump/. [On January 1, 2018, the corporate tax rate was lowered from 35 percent to 21 percent, and Apple repatriated some of its offshore money.]

Landlord Documents

(What San Francisco landlords wish they could give prospective tenants)

Pre-application to Lease

1) Are you over 27 years of age?

   Yes _____   No _____

2) Is your co-signer's minimum net worth at least $1,000,000?

   Yes _____   No _____

3) Are you in favor of rent control?

   Yes _____   No _____

4) Are you now, or have you ever, been a member of the Democratic Party?

   Yes _____   No _____

| _____ | _____ |
| Tenant Applicant | Date |

If you answered "yes" to any of these questions your application to rent is hereby denied.

Commentary:

1. If you are over 27 years of age, in a rent-controlled city, the risk to a landlord is that you'll settle down and start a family. The risk is you'll never leave the apartment. In ten years, the rent will be so low that you will have provided yourself a guaranteed retirement income—at the expense of the landlord who is subsidizing your apartment for life.

2. A rent payment, like a mortgage payment, shouldn't be more than 25 percent of your earnings. If your one-bedroom apartment rents for $4,000 a month, you should be earning $16,000 a month. You don't, hence, the cosignatory requirement.

3. If you favor rent control, you will complain to the San Francisco Rent Board whenever something is not to your liking (rather than discuss it with your landlord), and the board will rule in your favor.

4. If you are a card-carrying member of the Democratic Party, you will vote for even stricter rent control laws maybe even sales control laws.

Preamble to Lease

Dear Tenants:

Welcome to San Francisco. Like the city's expansive views, tenants in San Francisco enjoy expansive rights. Take your newfound rights seriously. They have immediate cash value.

To best determine your new rights and their approximate cash value, consult an attorney. Search "tenant attorneys," or go directly to the Tenderloin Housing Clinic. You will pay nothing at this time. Tenant services are free. Attorneys charge only if they obtain a judgment in your favor. (This is automatic, but you'll have to split the reward with the attorney.)

All San Francisco government agencies advocate on your behalf. The most active are the San Francisco Department of Public Health, Department of Building Inspection, and Rent Board. Visit these agencies as soon as possible. They will help you build a case.

Caution: if the building subject to this lease was built after 1976, you are forfeiting rights and privileges. You are forfeiting, for example, the right to declare your building uninhabitable (for the purpose of not paying rent), forfeiting the right to ask your friends to move in (to help pay the rent, later, the entire rent), and the right to reject a rent raise. Why? Because buildings built after 1976 are not subject to rent control.

In other words, choose your apartment well; it may be for life. Because San Francisco landlords raise rents as high as they can whenever there is a vacancy, your next apartment will be unaffordable. (As a tenant, consider joining a tenant union to get this outrageous law changed.)

ACKNOWLEDGED:

_____   _____
          Tenant   Date

_____   _____
         Landlord   Date

Lease Addendum

In January 2004, the San Francisco Board of Supervisors announced that except in a public safety emergency, even casual verbal discussion between landlord and tenant is harassment of the tenant. Be advised, then, that communication between landlord and tenant shall be through attorneys only.

WARNING:

Earthquakes in San Francisco are commonplace. Chances are the building will collapse and kill you. Landlord does not warrant the building is seismically safe. Tenant rents at his or her own risk!

Building is and probably will always be out of compliance with current building codes for new construction. Landlord warrants habitability only as per building codes at the time of the building's construction (100 years ago).

You, as well as other tenants, will be sneaking in new roommates (which the Rent Board ruled is not ground for eviction) without landlord approval. Landlord hereby warns that there are probably psychopaths living in the building. Again, tenant rents at his or her own risk!

ACKNOWLEDGED AND APPROVED:

_____   _____
              Tenant   Date

_____   _____
        Tenant's Attorney   Date

_____   _____
            Landlord   Date

Termination of Lease Agreement

Tenant hereby voluntarily terminates his residency. In consideration, landlord agrees to pay a termination fee based on the following San Francisco Buyout Formula:

Market Rent + 10%, less Current Rent, X 24

Example:

$3,500 market rent
+ $350 (10%) =
$3,850
-$1,500 current rent =
$2,350
x 24 months =
$56,400 Total Buyout

Tenant hereby agrees to hold landlord harmless with respect to any future claim of unjust enrichment or violation of the Residential Rent Stabilization and Arbitration Ordinance.

AGREED and ACKNOWLEDGED:

_____   _____
Tenant   Date

_____   _____
Landlord   Date

Prospective Juror Number 26
or
Jury Shock: A Tale of Dismissal

In a San Francisco criminal court, the following was asked of a public school teacher by the defense attorney:

"Prospective juror number twenty-six, are you able to set aside your own experiences to impartially judge the facts in this case? You've heard other prospective jurors testify that they have witnessed or experienced unacceptable social behavior—harassment while taking public transportation, a mugging at gunpoint—plus you will hear testimony by the prosecuting attorney that the defendant was involved with drugs. Can you put all of that aside to consider the facts, namely that the defendant allegedly was unnecessarily roughed up by the arresting police, and that because they were undercover, were not wearing uniforms, the confused defendant fought back in self-defense, something anyone might have done? Prospective juror number twenty-six, can you judge the facts impartially?"

"Oh, most definitely!" replied PJN26. "I'll be very evenhanded."

In such a liberal city as San Francisco, where citizens are so used to antisocial behavior, and in the name of "social justice" so accustomed to local government skewing social, political and economic affairs, should attorneys even ask such a question? The fact that the defendant may not even take the stand because it's up to the prosecution to prove that he's guilty is also disturbing.

The problem in San Francisco is that when citizens find themselves in a court of law, where they are sworn to respond honestly, they cannot just put aside their experiences. When the purpose of a court of law is to confront those experiences, confront tort, confront the negative consequences of lax law enforcement and, where prospective jurors are asked to acknowledge, publicly, as part of the jury selection process, unacceptable social behavior they personally experienced, there is a problem. It is why, in San Francisco, trial attorneys accept jurors who are less than impartial.

When asked whether they had any experiences that might affect their decision in the case, every prospective juror responded with, "Yes."

———————

Why was prospective juror number 26 turned away? The defendant's attorney seemed quite pleased with his response; PJN26 assumed he would be chosen. The court clerk then called out, "Will prospective juror number twenty-six please go to jury seat number four." About to gather his belongings, the prosecuting attorney interrupted with, "The court would like to thank and dismiss prospective juror number twenty-six." The entire courtroom burst into laughter, including the judge. It was only afterward that PJN26 realized that if the defense counsel seemed so pleased with his response, the prosecuting counsel could not possibly have been. In fact, prosecuting counsel couldn't wait to get rid of number 26—having long ago written "NO" on his yellow Post-it note.

In the courtroom hallway, PJN26 proclaimed to PJN12, the brother of a police officer who had also been dismissed, "I knew they would dismiss you, but I can't understand why they dismissed me." To which PJN12 responded, "From the moment you opened your mouth, *everyone* knew that *you* were history. In life, it's not just what you say, it's also *how* you say it."

George Floyd

No one is above the law also means no one is below the law. Justice must be blind.

Was George Floyd an ordinary citizen? Irrelevant. The police killing was racist murder.

———————

Underlying reality:

1. African-Americans commit 36 percent of all crime; they comprise 12 percent of the population.[78]

2. Police put their lives on the line every day to deal with crime on the streets—in contrast to their own lives in their own neighborhoods. After 20 years, do they end up disliking the people they are dealing with? Perhaps no officer should be on the street more than 20 years (as should no social worker or inner-city school teacher). They are at risk of roughing up their suspects, though Harvard professor Steven Pinker warns not to confuse unnecessary police harassment of African-Americans with police murder of African-Americans. No one denies the harassment rate is way out of proportion. The murder rate is not.[79] Proportionately, just as many Blacks are shot by Black officers as by white. Shortly after the Floyd murder, the *New York Times* reported three more police killings of Blacks, all by Black officers.

3. George Floyd was not an ordinary citizen. A very large Black man,[80] a convicted felon, a drug user, known to have committed numerous serious crimes including holding a gun to a pregnant woman, he resisted arrest.

---

[78] United States Department of Justice Statistics, Bureau of Justice, "Race and Ethnicity of Violent Crime Offenders and Arrestees, 2018," Alan J. Beck, Washington, DC, January 2021, https://bjs.ojp.gov/library/publications/race-and-ethnicity-violent-crime-offenders-and-arrestees-2018.

[79] Ronald Bailey, "Steven Pinker Survives Attempted Cancellation," *Reason*, October 2020, p. 71, https://reason.com/2020/09/06/steven-pinker-survives-attempted-cancellation/.

[80] Jesse Jackson once said something like, "I was walking alone down an alley at night when I heard two men following me. I said to myself, Oh, shit. When they got near, I turned to confront them. Man, was I relieved when I saw they were white."

175

4. Vicious police are attracted to "liberal" cities. Why? Liberal cities are lax on law enforcement, on forbidding homeless from living on the sidewalks, on pursuing theft, on pursuing rioters who loot and vandalize.[81] Plus their public prosecutors are as concerned with the rights, needs and humanity of those who perpetrate crime as they are with their victims. This underlying reality creates citizens not really wanting to know what their police departments are doing, how police are trained, what they are required to do. But *that* is what attracts the most vicious police from around the nation to San Francisco, Minneapolis, New York and Los Angeles, cities known for their rough policing tactics.

———

Before the trial, the underlying reality was that the officer in the George Floyd killing might have gone free. The law is clear: police are not accountable when, in a life-threatening situation, even if it's only in their own mind, an officer makes a split-second decision that is wrong.

California

The sheen is wearing off the Golden State. We don't notice because the state is so prosperous, but decades of high taxes, burdensome regulations and government mismanagement have had their effect. California's prosperity is due to factors that have so far eluded the

---

[81] "Peaceful civil-rights demonstrations are too easily ignored, whereas riots and looting are more effective at attracting attention to a cause. The shared experience of looting can also be Joyous, produce community cohesion, and count as a small act of direct redistribution of wealth." Vicky Osterweil, *In Defense of Looting: A Riotous History of Uncivil Action (Bold Type Books, 2020);* in *The Economist,* "Smash and Grab: Chicago, Civil Unrest and Inequality," August 15, 2020, https://www.economist.com/united-states/2020/08/13/chicago-civil-unrest-and-inequality.

state's grip—notably that California is a world center of artificial intelligence, nanotechnology, information technology, biological engineering, electric automobiles, and space exploration, all of which attract entrepreneurs and start-ups from around the world, which means California's 21st-century economy thrives in spite of California's negative economic restraints. For now.

With their salaries so high, those working in science and technology can ignore the Bay Area's soaring property prices. Bay Area millennials can remain ignorant of the fact that those prices are a direct response to the economic negatives. But modest income and minority populations cannot. *They* pay those high property prices, attend those low-performing public schools, experience poor public services, and outside of high tech, endure low levels of job creation.

Here are some facts:

- California ranks 49th in the nation in unemployment,[82] 49th in the cost of doing business, and 50th for business friendliness.[83]

- In its annual survey of CEOs, *Chief Executive* magazine ranked California as the worst place to do business. The state has received the lowest ranking each year since the magazine began its survey in 2004. *US News and World Report* ranks California 50th for opportunity.[84]

---

[82] U.S. Bureau of Labor Statistics, TED: The Economics Daily, "Unemployment Rates Lower in 49 States and DC From June 2020 to June 2021, Washington, DC, July 23, 2021, https://www.bls.gov/opub/ted/2021/unemployment-rates-lower-in-49-states-and-dc-from-june-2020-to-june-2021.htm.

[83] Evan Harris, "California's Business Climate Continues to Receive Poor Scores," July 16, 2019, https://www.pacificresearch.org/californias-business-climate-continues-to-receive-poor-scores/.

[84] "Best States Rankings," *US News & World Report*, 2021, https://www.usnews.com/news/best-states.

- California's unfunded pension liabilities for cities, counties and the state total $1.5 trillion (as of June 2017).[85]

- Nationwide, California's educational system is ranked 40th.[86]

- With only 12 percent of the nation's population, California is home to 33 percent of the nation's welfare recipients.[87]

Is this important? Not if there are offsetting factors that contribute to the state's prosperity. Reality, however, is that the working middle class pays for *all* the state's economic restraints, for example, pays property taxes then pays again to send their children to private schools. Unlike the poor and rich who understand the link between public schools, public housing and public prisons, the middle class thinks it has no choice but to continue paying for such a rotting system. Was the late California historian, Kevin Starr, wrong, then, when he declared: "California is on the verge of becoming the first failed state in America"? Was British Prime Minister Margaret Thatcher wrong when she declared: "The trouble with socialism is that eventually you run out of other people's money"?

———

What's to be done? To significantly lower costs, former Governor Arnold Schwarzenegger tried to turn some of California's services

[85] Marc Joffe and Edward Ring, "*California's State and Local Liabilities Total $1.5 Trillion,*" California Policy Center, January 3, 2019, https://californiapolicycenter.org/californias-state-and-local-liabilities-total-1-5-trillion-2/.

[86] Brett Ziegler, "Education Rankings," *US News & World Report, 2021,* https://www.usnews.com/news/best-states/rankings/education.

[87] Kerry Jackson (Pacific Research Institute fellow), "California, Poverty Capital," *City Journal*, Winter 2018, https://www.city-journal.org/html/california-poverty-capital-15659.html.

over to the private sector. He couldn't. Entrenched self-serving political interests prevented it.

How did that come about? When the nation turned to government to solve its problems. It started in the 1930s when President Franklin Roosevelt initiated a pile of programs. Those programs will never be reversed. Here are a few:

AAA   Agricultural Adjustment Administration (farm subsidies)
CCC   Civilian Conservation Corps (employment)
CWA   Civilian Works Administration (employment)
WPA   Works Progress Administration (employment)
PWA   Public Works Administration (employment)
FERA   Federal Emergency Relief Administration (employment paid for with federal loans to the states)
NRA   National Recovery Administration (control of industry, support of unions)
FDIC   Federal Deposit Insurance Corporation (government insurance of bank deposits)
AFDC   Aid to Families with Dependent Children (added to the Social Security Act)

Congress vetoed all these programs as unconstitutional. Roosevelt then threatened to pack the Supreme Court with six additional justices to approve those programs—the socialist agenda of the day, adopted by Germany, Italy and Japan. Like Hitler, Stalin and the Emperor, Roosevelt eliminated the opposition, in his case, the Constitution. According to Chief Justice Benjamin Cardozo, Roosevelt absolutely frightened the court into submission.

Federal spending, historically 3 percent of GDP (except during periods of war), rose to 12 percent by 1940, 17 percent by 1950, 28 percent from 1980 on.

None of this was envisioned by the framers of the Constitution. Taxation to pay for federal grants-in-aid to the states and local governments, federal transfer payments to individuals—

none of that. In 1964, another megalomaniac, Lyndon Baines Johnson, gave us the War on Poverty:

Economic Opportunity Act
    Volunteers in Service to America (VISTA);
    Job Corps; Head Start; Legal Services;
    Community Action Program

Food Stamp Act

Elementary and Secondary Education Act

Social Security Act
    Medicare, Medicaid, and a huge increase in
    Social Security payouts

The underlying fact, however, is that the needle barely budged. Poverty was 15 percent in 1964 and has remained on average around 13 percent, fluctuating between 11 and 15 percent.[88] Withdraw federal programs now, and immediately, poverty increases to 22 percent.[89]

Who is responsible for this? The Democratic Party. Democrats have created the illusion that they saved the nation from the Great Depression.[90] Democrats create the illusion they save the poor from poverty, especially the Black community. According to Elbert Guillory, state senator from Louisiana, Black, Democrats have created the illusion that big government is what ensures social justice for all Americans. Except to Guillory, big government is really about *control*. In the name of charity, it offers welfare—not designed to lift

---

[88] UC Davis Center for Poverty Research (2015).

[89] Latent poverty is an additional seven percent. Charles Murray, *Losing Ground: American Social Policy, 1950-1980* (Basic Books, 1984), p.65.

[90] The Great Depression ended in 1933 exactly when Roosevelt's programs kicked in. Those programs reversed the ending. Unemployment immediately jumped from 15 to 25 percent, and the Depression continued an additional eight years. [Depressions never last more than four years. The Great Depression lasted 11 because government intervened, a historical first. The Great Recession of 2008, thanks to government intercession, lasted 10 years instead of two.]

Black Americans out of poverty but to convince Black Americans that they need government to get ahead in life. This is why Guillory calls Democrats limousine liberals, the nation's new plantation owners who do nothing to encourage Black self-reliance; who, to the contrary, sacrifice Black self-reliance to their new overseers—left-wing politicians who control constituents by making them dependent.[91]

Elbert Guillory is a Republican in Louisiana, the South, where being Republican is normal—where Alveda King, niece of Martin Luther King Jr., is a Republican. In California, being a Republican is not normal, where the Republican Party is largely moribund. Yet, incongruously, California is the intellectual center of American conservatism:

Cato Institute (San Francisco, moved to Washington, DC)

Independent Institute (Oakland)

Pacific Research Institute (San Francisco)

Hoover Institute (Stanford University)

Claremont Institute (Upland, Southern California)

Center for Right-Wing Studies (Berkley, California)

And California is the birthplace of radical conservative laws:

Prop 13 (property tax limited to one percent of a property's purchase price)

---

[91] Elbert Guillory, "Senator Elbert Guillory on Switching from Democrat to Republican," interview, by John Caldara of the Independence Institute (Denver), *YouTube,* 13:09, December 29, 2015, https://www.youtube.com/watch?v=e-xBgfDdfAg, in which Guillory notes that Lyndon Johnson himself said, when he signed the 1964 Civil Rights Act, "I'm going to give them just enough to keep them quiet, not enough to make a difference, and I will have those [racial epithet] voting Democrat for the next 200 years." To Guillory, that statement encapsulates the Democratic Party, why "The Black community should not have put all its eggs in one basket."

Prop 209 (ban on affirmative action, the California Civil Rights Initiative)

Prop 187 (prohibition of illegal aliens using state health, education and other services)

These laws have been totally or partially repealed because the liberal culture in California has been able to portray Republicans as bigots. Proof: voter registration decreased from 40 percent Republican in 1990 to 25 percent in 2017.

And California was the battleground in "The Resistance" to Donald Trump. The state prevented such speakers as Ann Coulter, Milo Yiannopoulos and Ben Shapiro from addressing students at University of California campuses. In California, the ACLU no longer unequivocally defends free speech.

———

In America there is a cultural war. Currently, forces of the Left are prevailing over those of the Right, although not in national politics.

Europe (with a few exceptions) does not have this war, nor is it likely to in the future since there is no social force of any significance that could launch an offensive against the Left's cultural monopoly. It's only a matter of time before the Left completely takes over America:

> America can't succeed unless *you* succeed. That is why I am running for president of the United States. Here on Roosevelt Island, I believe we have a continuing rendezvous with destiny. Each American and the country we cherish. I'm running to make our economy work for you and for every American.
> —Hillary Clinton, June 13, 2015, New York City, Roosevelt Island[92]

---

[92] Andrew Prokop, "Transcript: Hillary Clinton's Official Campaign Launch Speech," www.vox.com, June 13, 2015, https://www.vox.com/2015/6/13/8776067/hillary-clinton-transcript-campaign-launch.

A perfect speech. Absolutely no message. Clinton knew to say nothing. When you presume that Americans believe that Republicans are evil, and in her case that Donald Trump was so unqualified for the presidency that she would win by default, no message is necessary. But that allowed Donald Trump to reduce his message to "Make America Great Again" and to present himself as the radical candidate for "Hope and Change."

Had she a relevant message, Clinton would have won. Had any of the Republican candidates a message, they would have defeated Trump in the primaries. Had Mitt Romney displayed any human warmth, he would have brought Barack Obama presidency to an end after only four years in the 2012 election and won again in 2016. Donald Trump could not, then, have astounded himself and the nation in his run for the presidency.

Girls of the Golden West

December 3, 2017

John Adams
c/o San Francisco Opera
301 Van Ness Avenue
San Francisco, CA 94102

Dear Mr. Adams:

The opening line of your opera, *Girls of the Golden West*, commissioned and premiered in San Francisco, is, "We are a unique group of people." Spoken by a miner, that line, a token gesture to the possibility that California's greatness stems from the hope and optimism of the Gold Rush, was abandoned in favor of the opera's real message: to show the dark side of that period, how, for example, minorities of color were badly treated. That incessant one-sided portrayal left audience members who stayed to the opera's end with the feeling: "I hate America."

The only audience, then, who will ever attend the opera a second time will be recent graduates of American colleges. Having learned American history according to Howard Zinn, they will be sympathetic to the opera's purpose. The bulk of today's opera audience, older, will never be.

Why center a work of art on political ideology, on waning Left-wing postmodernism? Once that ideology is discredited, no one will want to see such a dated opera. In the program notes, you describe yourself as a composer, a conductor and creative thinker. You shouldn't say anything. Let the music speak for itself. Let the singers sing in *solfège*.

And then, why has this reviewer, after repeated listening to your works, never felt a spiritual connection? Is it because your self-conscious philosophy so permeates the music and is so distracting that it prevents the listener from experiencing your works as art? With repetition evoking Steve Reich, *Girls of the Golden West* comes off as lecture. If spirituality is a release from consciousness, why make the listener so hyper-conscious?

Things to Do Around San Francisco

By Gary Snyder[93]

Catch eels in the rocks below the Palace of the Legion of Honor.[94]

Four in the morning—congee at Sam Wo.[95]

Walk up and down Market, upstairs playing pool,

Turn on at Aquatic Park — seagulls steal bait sardine

Going clear out to Oh's to buy bulghur.[96]

Howard Street Goodwill

Not paying traffic tickets; stopping the phone.

Merry-go-round at the beach, the walk up to the cliff house,

sea lions and tourists—the old washed-out road that goes on—

Play chess at Mechanics'[97]
Dress up and go looking for work[98]

Seek out the Wu-t'ung trees park arboretum.

Suck in the sea air and hold it—miles of white walls—sunset shoots
back from somebody's window high in the Piedmont hills

---

[93] David Lehman, ed., *The Oxford Book of American Poetry* (Oxford University Press, 2006).

[94] In the 1960s, this author did these things and thought: "This is the good life, San Francisco, Haight-Ashbury, quite the hippy village." Not unrelated is Tony Bennett's version of "It's the Good Life." Listen to the words; life is not about acquiring material things, the "beat" message, why Tony also sang, "I Left My Heart in San Francisco."

[95] Restaurant deep in Chinatown. No longer opposite the neon "Buddha Bar" sign, no longer the tiny turning staircase to march three flights up, at 4 a.m., to be greeted by rude waiter Edsel (who everyone enjoyed because we knew we deserved it, having just read *The Ugly American*), who then pulled up our order via the dumbwaiter after hearing the kitchen yell "congee" (rice porridge). The crowd today, employees from the TransAmerica Building across the street, come at 4 p.m.

[96] Oh's Fine Foods, bulk dry goods, Mission Street.

[97] Mechanics' Institute, a private library (where, in part, this book was written): two floors of books (after two flights of walk-up), then the third-floor international chess center.

[98] A childish understanding.

Get drunk all the time. Go someplace and score.

Walk in and walk out of the Asp[99]

Hike up Tam[100]

Keep quitting and starting at Berkeley

Watch the pike in the Steinhart Aquarium: he doesn't move.

Sleeping with strangers

Keeping up on the news

Chanting sutras after sitting

Practicing yr frailing on guitar

Get dropped off in the fog in the night

Fall in love twenty times

Get divorced

Keep moving—move out to the Sunset[101]

Get lost _____ or

 Get found[102]

(1966)

---

[99] The Anxious Asp, a café whose bathroom was wallpapered with *The Kinsey Reports*; was the center of the birth of the Beats, 1961 (later became Vesuvio's, now a tourist attraction, but not totally). Jack Kerouac lived upstairs.

[100] Mount Tamalpais, in Marin County, across the Golden Gate Bridge.

[101] Sunset District, mostly man-produced, affordable homes, runs along the west side of Golden Gate Park from the Upper Haight to the Pacific Ocean. The Outer Sunset is today, "Outer Lands," home of our "millennial beats."

[102] One side of this author, nostalgic for this era, still drops by City Lights Bookstore, which I did regularly when my band played regularly across the street at the Purple Onion comedy club (until that club closed for good), just like the hungry i, also a North Beach music and stand-up comedy club and birthplace of such comedians as Mort Sahl, Lenny Bruce, Woody Allen, the Smothers Brothers, Phyllis Diller, Robin Williams.

After the Cries of the Birds

By Lawrence Ferlinghetti[103]

Hurrying thru eternity
after the cries of the birds has stopped
I see the "future of the world"
in a new visionary society
now only dimly recognizable
in folk-rock ballrooms
free-form dancers in ecstatic clothing
their hearts their gurus[104]
every man his own myth
butterflies in amber
caught fucking life
hurrying thru eternity
to a new pastoral era[105]
I see the shadows of that future
in that white island
which is San Francisco
floating in its foreign sea
seen high on a hill
in the Berkeley Rose Garden
looking West at sunset to the Golden Gate
adrift in its Japanese landscape
under Mt. Tamal-Fuji

---

[103] Lawrence Ferlinghetti, *The Secret Meaning of Things* (New Directions Books, 1968).

[104] A guru is a personal, religious and spiritual guide in Hinduism, or an intellectual guide in matters of fundamental concern. If your heart is your guru, then you are Dionysus: emotion, romantic, the opposite of Apollo: reason, classical.

[105] Jean-Jacques Rousseau believed that people in a state of nature were innocent and at their best, then, corrupted by the unnaturalness of civilization. Twentieth-century civilization experienced the murder of 100 million people, but that is a drop in the bucket compared to the murder rate of uncivilized man in a state of nature, where the raiding of neighboring villages included the killing of all men, women, and children. Before the Jews were allowed to enter Israel, Moses ordered the complete annihilation of the people of Canaan. Deuteronomy 7.

with its grazing bulls
hurrying thru heaven
the city with its white buildings
"a temple to some unknown god"
(as Voznesensky said)
after the cries of the birds has stopped
I see the sea come in
over South San Francisco
and the island of the city
truly floated free at last
never really a part of America[106]
East East and West West
and the twain met long go
in "the wish to pursue what lies beyond the mind"
and with no place to go but In
after Columbus recovered America
and the West Coast captured by some Spanish Catholics
cagily getting the jump by sea
coveredwagons crawling over lost plains
hung up in Oklahoma
Prairie schooners into Pullmans
while whole tribes of Indians
shake hopeless feather lances
and disappear over the horizon
to reappear centuries later
feet up and smoking wild cigars
at the corner of Hollywood & Vine
hurrying thru eternity
must we wait for the cries of the birds
to be stopped
before we dig In
after centuries of running
up & down the Coast of West
looking for the right place to jump off

---

[106] San Franciscans always ask, about the rest of the nation, "Who are these people?"

further Westward
the Gutenberg Galaxy[107] casts its light no further
the "Westward march of civilization"
comes to a dead stop on the shores of
Big Sur Portland & Santa Monica
and turns upon itself at last
after the cries of the birds has stopped
must we wait for that
to dig a new model
of the universe
with instant communication
a world village
in which every human being is a part of us
 though we be still throw-aways
in an evolutionary progression[108]
as Spengler reverses himself[109]
Mark Twain meets Jack London

---

[107] *Gutenberg Galaxy, the Making of Typographical Man* by Marshall McLuhan (University of Toronto Press, 1962), claims that print technology modified the form of our perception, shifting and concentrating perceptual emphasis from the ear to the eye, with tremendous consequences for individuals and cultures.

[108] When you're young, if you don't think from the heart, if you're not liberal, something is wrong with you. When you're older and you still think from the heart, something is wrong with you. You didn't learn anything. Namely, that life is not a community of well-meaning human beings. Life is species in nature, genes adrift in space. Through leadership, we cannot progress beyond what evolution has brought. There are no species on Earth where leaders tell others what to do, where the community gets together and collectively creates its society. A bee colony is not a collective. Every bee knows what to do without being told. Like morality, everything we know is encoded in our genes. Instinct.

[109] Oswald Spengler, 1880–1836, German historian and philosopher, in *The Decline of the West* (1918-22), maintained that every culture passes a life cycle from youth through maturity and old age to death—and that the West had entered the period of decline from which there is no escape. The "Beats" identified with that. They lived that thought: "Look what capitalist materialism is doing to us; we can't take it; we're beat." In 1957, when Sputnik was launched, a Russian journalist living in California added the suffix "nik" to "beat," thus, "beatnik." (Some believe Herb Caen coined the word.)
The idea of a declining West underlies why so many people throughout the world (especially in the 1950s) looked to communism. It was the world's salvation: communal versus private, generosity versus selfishness, liberal versus conservative. Ferlinghetti wrote "After the Cries of the Birds" while in Moscow, soaking up the source of this salvation.

and turns back to Mississippi[110]
shaking his head
and the Last Frontier
having no place to go but In
can't face it
and buries its head
Western civilization gone too far West
might suffer a sea-change
into Something Else Eastern
and that won't do
The Chinese are coming anyway
time we prepared their tea[111]
Gunga Din still with us
Kipling nods & cries *I told you so!*[112]
The French King hollers *Merde!*
And abandons his Vietnam bordel
But not us
we love them too much for that
though the Mayflower turned around sets sail again
back to Plymouth England (and the Piltdown letdown)[113]
misjudging the coast & landing in Loverpool
American poets capture Royal Albert Hall
The Jefferson Airplane takes off
and circles heaven
It all figures

---

[110] Ferlinghetti is so wrapped up in anti-Westernism that he dismisses Mark Twain, whose *Huckleberry Finn* is arguably America's finest novel after Herman Melville's *Moby Dick*, in favor of San Francisco's (actually Oakland's) popular fiction writer, socialist Jack London.

[111] The Chinese must be gloating as they count the days before we *will* be pouring their tea. Thank you, naïve San Franciscans, for helping to make this happen.

[112] "Gunga Din" is an 1890 poem by Rudyard Kipling set in British India. The poem is remembered for its final line: "You're a better man than I am, Gunga Din."

[113] The Piltdown Man was a paleoanthropological fraud in which bone fragments were presented as the fossilized remains of a previously unknown early human. Referring to the Pilgrims, Ferlinghetti is again asking, "Who *are* these people?" A fraud? They're not *my* fellow Americans.

in a new litany
probably pastoral
after the cries of the birds has stopped
Rose petals fall in the Berkeley Rose Garden
where I sit trying to remember
the lines about rose leaves
in the **Four Quartets**[114]
Stella kisses her lover in the sunset
under an arbor
A Los Angeles actor nearby goes **Zap! Zap!**
at the setting sun
It is the end
I drop downhill
into a reception for Anaïs Nin
with a paperbag full of rose leaves
She is autographing her Book
I empty the bag over her head from behind
Her gold lacquered hair sheds the petals
They tumble red & yellow on her signed book
Girl again she presses them between the leaves
delightedly
like fallen friends
Her words
flame in my heart
Virginia Woolf under water
she drifts away on the book
a leaf herself blowing skittered

---

[114] The opening epigraph to *A San Francisco Conservative* is the opening to *Four Quartets*, in which T. S. Eliot states that time past, present, and future are the same. To conservatives, this is the most fundamental statement of conservatism. Ferlinghetti may not have known that, but would have known that 5th century Athens, 1st century Rome, were light-years more sophisticated than 20th century America. Why, instead of mocking Western civilization, he should have referenced its best: Socrates, Plato, Aristotle, Thucydides, Cicero, Tacitus, Horace, Pliny the Elder, Pliny the Younger.

over the horizon[115]
The wish to pursue what lies beyond the mind
lies just beyond
Ask a flower what it does
to move beyond the senses
Our cells hate metal
The tide turns
We shoot holes in the clouds' trousers
and napalm sears the hillsides
skips a bridge
narrows to a grass hut full of charred bodies
and is later reported looking like
"The eternal flame at Kennedy's grave"
A tree flowers red It can't run
Shall we now advance into the 21st century?
I see the lyric future of the world
on the beaches of Big Sur
gurus at Jack's Flats[116]
nude swart maidens swimming
in pools of sunlight
Kali on the beach[117]
guitarists with one earring
lovely birds in long dresses and Indian headbands
What does this have to do with Lenin?
Plenty![118]

---

[115] The Beat poets were young. At 19, everyone has youthful impulses, this author included —except the writings of Ginsburg and Kerouac, geniuses, will endure, while this well-written poem by this nostalgic commentator and San Francisco progressivism may not.

[116] Bixby Creek Canyon at Big Sur where Jack Kerouac wrote *Big Sur* while staying in Lawrence Ferlinghetti's secluded cabin.

[117] "Kali," the feminine form of Sanskrit "kala," time, doomsday, death (or black) is associated with "tantra," an ancient Indian practice that dates back more than 5,000 years. In Sanskrit the word tantra means woven together. People who practice Buddhist and Hindu meditation may also practice tantric sex as a way to "weave" the physical with the spiritual (exploring the body of another person). Whew! Those were the days!

[118] Nothing! The poem was written while Ferlinghetti was in Moscow imagining a world that doesn't exist.

Die-hard Maoists lie down together crosswise
and out comes a string
of Chinese firecrackers
and after the cries of the birds
has stopped
Chinese junks show up suddenly
off the coast of Big Sur
filled with more than Chinese philosophers
dreaming they are butterflies
How shall we greet them?[119] Are we ready
to receive them?
Shall we put out koan steppingstones
scrolls & bowls
greet them with *agape[120]*
Tu Fu and bamboo flutes at midnight?
Big Sur junk meet
Chinese junk?
Will they ride the breakers into Bixby Cove?
Will they bring their women with them
Will we take them on the beach
like Ron Boise's lovers in Kama Sutra[121]
face them with Zen zazen & tea[122]
made from the dust of the wings
of butterflies dreaming
they're philosophers?
Or meet them with last war's tanks
roaring out of Fort Ord

---

[119] Shall we greet these gods as the Aztecs greeted Cortez?

[120] Complete love; love in all its forms.

[121] Ron Boise (1931-1966), American sculptor who worked primarily with sheet metal (often from junked cars) to create nude figures, large abstract pieces, and fanciful musical instruments. He first came to prominence when, in 1964, the San Francisco police seized his series of male and female figures engaged in sexual unions described in the Kama Sutra (ancient Indian Sanskrit text on sexuality, eroticism, emotional fulfillment in life).

[122] Zazen is the heart of Japanese Zen Buddhism. The aim is to just sit—and suspend all judgmental thinking—to slide into calm.

down the highways & canyons
shooting as they come
flame-throwers flaming jelly
into the Chinese rushes
under the bridge at Bixby?
The U.S. owns the highway but is Big Sur
in the USA?
San Francisco floats away
beyond the three-mile limit
of the District of Eternal Revenue[123]
No need to pay your taxes
The seas come in to cover us
Agape we are & agape we'll be

---

[123] San Francisco, sanctuary, San Francisco, "summer of love."

4

SELECTED WRITINGS

Labyrinths

My son loves labyrinths and can figure them out in ten seconds.

One day I drew him the most complicated labyrinth possible (it took me half an hour). He looked at it, looked at me, and in one second, solved it.

Government creates the most complicated legislation to control business activity. Consider the Dodd-Frank Financial Reform Act of 2010, or the Sarbanes-Oxley Act of 2002. How long did it take those in business to figure out how to go around?

One millisecond.

Why does government think it can control the Zen masters of business and finance when to the contrary, like a Bach fugue, restraint only leads them to produce greater art?

Tie Goes to the Runner

In baseball, why does tie go to the runner? Because when a single batter with a thin stick of wood manages to hit a tiny ball coming at 100 mph, against nine fielders with wide mitts who need only catch that ball, yet reaches base at the same time as the ball, in the spirit of fairness, we credit the batter.

In the 2000 presidential election, George Bush was the batter, Al Gore, the fielder. Gore, with nine advantages over Bush—sitting vice president, better educated, better debater, a 70-30 lead going into the campaign, with the best possible asset, backing of the nation's finest politician and most popular president, Bill Clinton— should never have let that race end in a tie.

George Bush, with only one thing going for him, good judgment, kept his mouth shut. No matter what the question, Bush responded with, "limited government." He let Gore do the talking and disassociate himself from Bill Clinton to show the world he could do it all by himself. He hoped Gore would go easy on him during the debates, *which he did*, expatiating about his own interests, the environment, rather than what the voters cared about.

Not only George Bush, but so, too, did the voters use good judgment. What should have been a Gore landslide turned into a statistical tie and, in politics as in baseball, yes, tie goes to the runner.

The Florida Recount

From quantum mechanics comes Heisenberg's Uncertainty Principle, which says that it is impossible to know both the position and velocity of a particle at the same time. The act of measuring one necessarily disturbs the other. With respect to the Florida recount (presidential election 2000), the process of measuring disturbed the counting. Hand measuring to decide whether the ballot had produced a hanging chad (A, by one corner; B, by two corners; C, by three corners; D, by four corners), a pregnant chad, or a dimpled chad, produced a different total each time.

The Supreme Court affirmed that no citizen can be denied the vote without due process, that Florida had to recount its votes—provided Florida could agree upon a basis for counting them. The reality of enforcing that decision lead to the counting being canceled. By the time the court made its announcement, there was not enough time before January 20th to devise a "certain" system of counting that would account for the uncertainty principle, thus prevent George Bush from appealing, from running out the clock.[1]

---

[1] Unlike Richard Nixon, who won the popular vote in the 1960 presidential election—but lost the electoral vote because citizens in Chicago voted twice (which no one has ever disputed)—and conceded to Jack Kennedy because he felt it not in the best interest of the nation to block an incoming presidency, Al Gore put his own interest first. He didn't care if the recount would take two years; he had prepared for this election his entire life. The nation was counting on him. When he lost, it went into a mourning still felt today.

Two Senators

There are two senators for each state: two for Wyoming with its population of 600,000, and two for California's 39,000,000. There is good reason for this:

The Constitution accounts for profound philosophic differences throughout the nation by making all states equal—in the Senate—and accounts for profound demographic differences by making all states unequal[2]—in the House, where Wyoming has one member, California 53.

In the 1700s and 1800s, Americans lived on the land. Their problems stemmed from the land: animals, planting, harvesting, nature. Self-reliant, citizens were politically conservative. By the 1900s, most Americans were living in cities, and their problems stemmed from the urban environment: close quarters, alienation, industrialization, pollution. Less confident in themselves, less confident in the market, Americans turned to government. Having lost what in 1835 Alexis de Tocqueville in *Democracy in America* regarded as America's finest quality, self-reliance, Americans turned liberal. Employing the political process to solve social and economic problems, socialism, America today is not what the Founding Fathers envisioned.

America today is like the rest of the world. It fears economic freedom, it fears living without government—why the whole world is strapped with Keynesian debt, why President Biden's response to the COVID-19 pandemic is to borrow, then liberally spend. The whole world is doing this. The whole world, however, is at risk of economic collapse.

Europe, the U.S. Japan, China, all still bailing out their nations from the 2008 financial recession, are now, in response to COVID-19, adding a trillion dollars to their national debts. Unlike the 2008 financial crisis bailout where the banks paid back their loans, under the COVID-19 bailout, not all citizens will pay back

---

[2] Similarly, one purpose of the Electoral College is to give a little extra voting power to the smaller states.

200

their loans. Where is the line on the U.S. 1040 Federal Income Tax Return that adds $500, $1,000 or more, depending on how much was received, for 20 years (then packaged as a U.S. Treasury bond)?

The only thing holding off world economic catastrophe is the U.S. Constitution: a one-page document that enables small states such as Wyoming, with its two senators, to counter the entire nation's, perhaps the entire world's progressive tyranny of the majority (a tyranny completely indifferent to national debt—in the U.S., $28 trillion *before* the COVID-19 bailout). *That's* how great and important the U.S. Constitution is.

Pope Francis Address to Congress, September 24, 2015[3]

1. "I am most grateful . . . to address . . . Congress in 'the land of the free and the home of the brave.' I would like to think that the reason for this is that I, too, am a son of this great continent."

Latin America and South America may be "homes of the brave," but they are not "lands of the free." A populist communal culture sees to that. The people of Cuba certainly are not free. With restrictions on business, and so much public debt, Venezuela, Argentina, Nicaragua are not free.

2. "A political society endures when it seeks to satisfy common needs by stimulating the growth of . . . those in situations of greater vulnerability or risk. Legislative activity is always based on care for the people."

No. The job of government is to protect life, liberty and property, not to employ politics to solve economic problems, for example, to redistribute income and wealth. Redistributing wealth from those who make an economy grow to those whose only ambition is to "just get a job" will not stimulate economic growth.

Americans are a creative self-reliant entrepreneurial people— a nation of immigrants who fled oppression: who left family, friends, culture and property for a chance opportunity to better their lives. They took the potentials of a New World here and grew the economy. America's natural resource is its people.

Americans understand that the pursuit of self-interest is the basis for the organization of society, that the invisible hand of self-interest is the force behind both individual initiative *and* cooperation,

[3]His Holiness Pope Francis, Visit to The Joint Session of The United States Congress, "Address of The Holy Father," September 24, 2015, www.vatican.va, https://www.vatican.va/content/francesco/en/speeches/2015/september/documents/papa-francesco_20150924_usa-us-congress.html.

the force behind moral behavior. It is *the* check on dishonesty. It is what causes no one to purchase your goods or services if you are thought to be dishonest—which means you die. See Adam Smith, *The Theory of Moral Sentiments*, *The Wealth of Nations*, and Bernard Mandeville, *The Fable of the Bees*. See also Leo Tolstoy, *Anna Karenin*, wherein the author writes how wasteful it is for citizens to take time from their own productive work to do work that others should do for themselves (and how hypocritical it is to provide services that the providers themselves would never use, such as low-income schools and health clinics).[4]

3. "You [Congress] are asked to protect, by means of law, the image and likeness fashioned by God on every human face."

That is beyond what Congress does. Plus, God fastens his image on *everything* that lives. All of nature is the image of God.

4. "These are men and women who [help] sustain the life of society. They generate solidarity by their actions, and they create organizations which offer a helping hand to those most in need."

Correct, but contradicts point 2. Replace "they" create organizations with "government" creates organizations, and you reaffirm the populism of point 2.

5. "Elderly persons are a storehouse of wisdom forged by experience who seek to . . . share their stories and their insights."

---

[4] Leo Tolstoy, *Anna Karenin* (Penguin Classics, 1954, reprinted 1977), p. 267.

As his character, Levin, states, "I imagine that no sort of activity is likely to be lasting if it is not founded on self-interest, that's a universal principle, a philosophical principle."

Correct. Edmund Burke advocated that society distinguish between reform and revolution, that nations not be so quick to overthrow their institutions (as in the French Revolution). Why? Because the vast quantity of information and experience compiled over centuries contained in those institutions are beyond any single person's ability to comprehend, let alone a government.

6. "No religion is immune from forms of individual delusion or ideological extremism. We must be attentive to every type of fundamentalism, whether religious or of any other kind."

But, the U.S. Constitution *is* absolutism in the protection of individual freedom. To uphold Constitutional principles over the practical and political demands of pragmatism—is that ideological extremism? Barack Obama, before and throughout his presidency, declared that he disliked ideologues, that he was a pragmatist, that it was his intention to solve problems (the Affordable Care Act, for example), that he would not let the Constitution stand in his way. (In part, the election of Donald Trump was voter reaction to that stance.)

7. "We must move forward together, as one, in a renewed spirit of fraternity and solidarity, cooperating generously for the common good."

The New Deal, Great Society, War on Poverty—it's been done. The U.S. has a $28 trillion national debt—to pay for social programs for the common good that merely cover over poverty.

8. "[T]he voice of faith . . . is a voice of fraternity and love, which tries to bring out the best in each person and in each society."

In equal measure, religion destroys and has destroyed society, fraternity and love.

9. "[D]emocracy is deeply rooted in the mind of the American people."

Democracy is rooted almost exclusively in the minds of the American people! Outside the British Commonwealth, no nation has a history of democracy that ever lasted more than 70 years—mostly since World War II.

10. "If politics must truly be at the service of the human person, it follows that it cannot be a slave to the economy."

According to Marx, everything is a slave to the economy. Marx is correct. However, also true is that social, political and economic freedom are inherently interconnected, meaning that if nations restrict one freedom, they restrict the other two. Citizens, if you don't defend the freedoms you dislike, you will find yourself unable to defend those you do like—the original stance of the American Civil Liberties Union.

11. "America continues to be a land of dreams."

America is the land of freedom, thus, opportunity, thus, dreams. In a free society, one's life, liberty and property are one's own. In a free society, there is voluntary cooperation, there is equality of opportunity, but there is not equality of outcome.

12. "[T]he rights of those who were here long before us were not always respected."

True, but if they had been respected, nothing would be different today. If those before us had had property rights, "we" would not have been able to take their land; we would have been forced to pay for it—which we would have. In fact, to guarantee that we acquired it, we would have paid far more than "they" would have thought it was worth. Why? Because "we" had a vision as to its long-term value.

13. "[The Golden] Rule points us in a clear direction. Let us treat others with the same passion and compassion with which we want to be treated."

But, illegal immigrants aren't applying; they're just walking in. My grandmother's sister applied. In 1939, she was the one waving from the boat, the *Saint Louis*, docked in Havana that was sent back to Europe. She died in Auschwitz. Why, all of a sudden, is it acceptable for immigrants to just skip the application process?

14. "[S]ociety can only benefit from the rehabilitation of those convicted of crimes."

As public policy, the question is: does the benefit outweigh the cost? How many rehabilitated criminals are there? Of the students who drop out of school, how many are rehabilitated? What is the success rate? See point 15.

15. ". . . I would encourage you to keep in mind all those people around us who are trapped in a cycle of poverty. They too need to be given hope."

Poverty was 15 percent in 1964. Today, $28 trillion of U.S. debt later, poverty is still 15 percent. Nor has the dropout rate from school or the rate of criminal recidivism changed. Should we wait until the U.S. debt is $56 trillion before declaring that we lost the war?

You cannot do for others what they have to do for themselves. One-on-one attention over a period of ten years might help. But we're not doing that.

16. "Business is a noble vocation, directed to producing wealth and improving the world . . . especially if it sees the creation of jobs. . ."

Absolute nonsense. Business is directed at producing goods and services. At its best, at its most creative, business destroys jobs. Entrepreneurially lead production is what creates prosperity.

17. "This common good also includes the earth . . . We need a conversation which includes everyone, since the environmental challenge we are undergoing, and its human roots, concern and affect us all."

Why a conversation that includes everyone? Who disagrees? Polluters need to stop; the world needs to remove carbon dioxide from the atmosphere.

18. "When countries which have been at odds resume the path of dialogue . . . new opportunities open up for all."

Islam was spread and has ever since been maintained by the sword. Sharia law, leaders as descendants of Mohammed, women as slaves, there is nothing to discuss. There is no dialogue in Islam.

19. "Why are deadly weapons being sold to those who plan to inflict untold suffering on individuals and society? . . . [I]t is our duty to confront the problem and to stop the arms trade."

Is it our duty, then, to stop drug trafficking, to ban handguns? How? Where there is demand, there will be supply. Are we to stop citizens from protecting themselves? Europeans did that in the 1930s, making it possible for Hitler to round up seven million and march them to their death.

20. "I would like to call attention to those family members who are the most vulnerable: the young. [W]e live in a culture which pressures young people not to start a family, because they lack possibilities for the future. Yet this same culture presents others with so many options that they, too, are dissuaded from starting a family."

True.

————————

The UN will soon announce its program beyond the Millennium Development Goals of 2000. Those new goals will be touted as "sustainable," but there will be no mention of how the West lifted itself out of poverty: free-market capitalism. Nowhere in the draft to the UN goals will the words "capital" and "credit" appear. They certainly did not appear in the speech by Pope Francis.

Gradually I Have Come to Appreciate Andrew Carnegie

I just finished reading *Andrew Carnegie*, all 801 pages.[5] I appreciate that the author, David Nasaw, did not draw conclusions for the reader. I drew my own.

Without education, by age 33, one doesn't become the wealthiest person in the world, arguably today, without an understanding of the most fundamental truths about money, politics, economics, and life.

Rather than reaffirm that truth, author David Nasaw focused inordinately on the extravagances in Carnegie's life compared to the life of his workers at Carnegie Steel, who were suffering 12-hour days, seven days a week, as if it were Carnegie's making.

The author apparently does not believe Carnegie himself: "The real enemy of labor is labor, not capital," unions that fail to do their job to compel *all* mills to institute an eight-hour day (or impel Congress to pass a law forbidding employers to require more than an eight-hour day). To Carnegie, until that occurred, workingmen must make the best of their lot—as Carnegie himself did when he was young. A penniless immigrant, he saw the 12-hour day as an incentive to rise, as in *Empire of Business*, he advised everyone to do: start at the bottom, but don't stay there.

It was precisely because Carnegie had not forgotten his roots that he was one of the few unionized steel mills. When forced to cancel the contract, despite all he had done for them in the past, his workers struck. Yet, Carnegie knew what he was doing; the 1892 Homestead Strike had to be broken. Carnegie had the most underlying truth—namely, that he would have lost future orders and market share to his nonunion competition. He would have had to abandon his business model, the basis of his success: no matter what the economy, *do not stop production!* Even at cost, take all orders; grab market share from those mills that cannot hold on.

When no one else did, Carnegie kept his workers employed during the Panic of 1873 because he did not stop production. And

---

5 David Nasaw, *Andrew Carnegie* (Penguin Press, 2006).

not about to during the Homestead Strike—with thousands of workers streaming in from Italy and Germany.

Carnegie's business model also consisted of reinvesting 75 percent of profits back into the mills, retrofitting, upgrading plants with the latest technology, constantly pushing for higher productivity, thus, lower prices. This is how Carnegie Steel remained competitive. Carnegie's fortune did not come from purposely underselling his competition to drive them out of business. It is why, to Carnegie, workers have no right to tell owners how to operate. Ayn Rand might have said, "Workers (or government) have no right to tell artists what to draw or how to draw."

Author Nasaw was fooling himself if he believes Carnegie lived in idle extravagance, indifferent to his suffering workers. Carnegie was making a point. He had the big picture.

He also had the big picture with respect to forces building up toward World War I. He devoted the last 20 years of his life to trying to prevent it. He sat down, one-on-one, with every U.S. president, every British prime minister, and with Kaiser Wilhelm, imploring them to stop stockpiling arms, building battleships. To Carnegie, like kids with guns, they would not be able to stop themselves from using them, that a minor incident would surely set off a world war. Exactly what happened.

He suggested Germany and Britain combine their navies, then use them to prevent war. The Carnegie Endowment for International Peace in Washington, DC, Moscow, Beirut, Beijing, Brussels, New Delhi is still in operation, still well-funded.

———————

The reason I read *Andrew Carnegie* was that earlier in my career, I had read *and applied* Carnegie's principles from *Empire of Business*. I was moved by his profound understanding of money and business. Now I've read *Gospel of Wealth*.

Subtle, poetry, those two books perfectly explain Andrew Carnegie. Why did the author of *Andrew Carnegie* not discuss them in depth? In a letter to the author, I congratulated him on not drawing conclusions for the reader, but as I have gradually come to appreciate Andrew Carnegie, I have come to realize that Nasaw had no conclusions—why he focused inordinately on silliness in Carnegie's personal life, and the fact that both Henry Clay Frick and every U.S. president (to whom the industrialist had immediate access) mocked him. Irrelevant. Look closely at any great person—there are always incongruities. Important is that *Empire of Business* and *Gospel of Wealth* reveal Carnegie's deep understanding not only of money, business and politics, but, also via Herbert Spencer, Darwin's *Survival of the Fittest* as it applies to the natural evolution of the advanced industrialized economy—with its concentration of wealth, creation of monopoly, then complete destruction.

Gospel of Wealth explains Carnegie's notion that those who know how great fortunes are made (not simply wealth) are the ones who should decide how great fortunes are spent, namely, on lasting public works, projects that enable citizens to improve themselves, projects that provide enjoyment for *all* members of society. Increasing worker's wages, giving alms to the poor, that only increases consumer spending, a temporary use, a permanent throwing of money to the wind.

Building libraries, concert halls, institutions that work for world peace—that's where money should go. Today, on medical research, preservation of open space, removal of CO_2 from the atmosphere.

————

Carnegie is criticized for his handling of the Homestead Strike. Not fair. To carefully distribute his fortune, at age 33, he had to retreat from Carnegie Steel. He knew only one person capable of replacing himself—Henry Clay Frick. Frick agreed, with one stipulation. Carnegie was not to step in whenever he pleased. It was Frick who called in the Pinkerton guards to keep striking workers from preventing replacement (scab) labor from entering the mill. Seven workers and three Pinkerton guards died; the strike lasted four months. Had he been in charge, Carnegie said he would have broken his own rule for a few days and stopped production. Considering his abhorrence of violence, with the latter part of his life spent trying to prevent war, that strike should not be substantially pinned on him. "Oh, yes, he gave us libraries, but he exploited his workforce to pay for them." Not true.

––––––––––

Underlying Carnegie's certainty was his solid belief, from his long conversations with social-economist Herbert Spencer, that the Industrial Revolution was an evolutionary step forward. Not exactly biological, but the change was real and here to stay. As the Big Bang burst the universe into existence, so, too, the Industrial Revolution burst the modern world into existence, at the onset of the 19th century—as the result of division of labor applied to mass production. In 1820, world per capita income was $605 a year. In 1920, $1382 a year; in 2010, $7890 a year.[6] With constant innovation in technology, with government keeping its hands off the economy, there is no limit to economic growth.[7]

In other words, before the Industrial Revolution, the world was communist: no one owned property, every man was economically and socially equal, poor, without rights, not participating in matters of state. Products were crude and prices high. With industrialization, quality rose and prices fell. Standard of living rose—dramatically.

As the advanced industrialized economy evolved naturally, so, too, did firms. To Carnegie, the more successful firms are at raising prices, the more likely they are to encourage *competition*— from firms selling similar goods at lower prices. In a competitive market, profit drops to zero (although management earns high

––––––––––

[6] van Zanden, J.L., et al. (eds.), *How Was Life?: Global Well-Being since 1820*, (OECD Publishing, 2014), doi: 10.1787/9789264214262-en. The per capita incomes are calculated in 1990 dollars.

[7] The Achilles' heel of a dynamic economy is that so much wealth is created that citizens no longer need to work—why consensus is building regarding implementing "universal basic income."

salaries). All cartels fail; all businesses fail.[8] Efficient Market Hypothesis.

Carnegie's grasp of the underlying truths of business, money, economics, and evolution enabled him not to waiver. With the Homestead Strike, he stuck to his business model.

Nineteenth-century Europe and America saw the evolution of advanced industrialized economies as justification for colonialism, a natural extension of survival of the fittest, their destiny, then, to appropriate the lives and resources of less-developed nations. At first, citizens of less-developed nations welcomed the intrusion, happy to have the jobs, happy to witness the development of their country. Later, they revolted. Today, however, some wonder if they weren't better off as colonies.

> For he that makes the best judgment of the truth of things, he that readily finds the way to't, and gives the best account of the reason of it, we conclude him, without all dispute, to be the wisest man.

—Cicero[9]

---

[8] Three of the top one hundred firms on the Dow Jones Industrial Average in 1961 exist today.

[9] Classics of Roman Literature, ed. Harry E. Wedeck (Rowman & Littlefield, 1963), p. 352.

A Conversation

David Parker: The market can handle all of society's problems. Society may not want the market to do that. Society may want a neutral third party to monitor, to regulate, but that neutral third party need not be government. Government may be the most convenient vehicle, but that's another matter.

Chris van Buren[10]: Certain aspects of civilization should not be market-driven, profit-driven. For example, private police or fire departments have no incentive to protect poor neighborhoods—until those in rich neighborhoods realize that fires in poor neighborhoods spread, and that maybe socialized fire protection is a good idea.

> [We agree, but for different reasons. **CVB** believes markets shouldn't provide certain services, period, because markets are incapable of providing them adequately. **DP** believes society doesn't want the market to provide certain services, but that the market is capable. All that's required is that services to the public, private or government, be monitored and be offered equally to all citizens.]

CVB: That implies bigger government. I thought you were against big government.

DP: No. That implies punishment—disobey, lose your license to operate.

> [We are both advocating for government, but **DP** believes that with consistent law enforcement,

---

10 Christopher Van Buren is a writer, publisher, literary agent, and correspondent for *U.S. Industry Today*. He is the president and CEO of LaunchMoxie, Inc., the premier digital marketing agency in the self-help and body-mind-spirit-Earth markets.

everyone gets the message (à la New York City),
and the crime level will drop—implying, thus,
fewer prisons and less government.]

CVB: Regulation implies big government to enforce the law.

DP: Regulation does not imply government. It implies agreed-upon regulators—which come just as easily from the private sector, UL, Underwriters Laboratories, for example, for electrical appliances. The American Medical Association for the medical profession.

CVB: Prisons for-profit have an incentive to increase the number of prisoners. More prisons, more profit. They will push [bribe] governments to incarcerate at a higher rate and for longer terms. Similarly, health industry for-profit has an incentive to keep people sick, to keep them longer in the hospital and require unnecessary but highly profitable surgery.

DP: A truism, not a complete explanation of reality. Where there is competition for services, firms have an incentive to provide the best possible service—to not receive bad reviews on the Internet. Firms are always at risk of no one wanting their services.

> [If the medical profession is nationalized, shouldn't
> the legal profession be nationalized? Lawyers arc
> notorious for dragging cases on forever, for profit.]

Such a truism is really fear of the market, an unJeffersonian belief that average citizens can't think for themselves, an elitist's underestimation of the people, and democracy, pure Plato's *Republic*.

CVB: Your comment implies that competition keeps the market honest. BUT WE DON'T HAVE PERFECT COMPETITION! Worse, we have big business that socializes its losses and privatizes its gains. Walmart workers are paid so poorly they are forced to live on food stamps—at public expense.

[We agree that's wrong.]

DP: It exists because most people in America live way beyond their means. Reality is that no one works for less than subsistence wage. True during the Industrial Revolution, true today.

CVB: During the Industrial Revolution and industrialization of America, you had corporations virtually enslaving their employees, including children, forcing them into company housing and buying their necessities from the company store. So they accumulated debt to the company that they could never fully work off. Labor Unions formed because people did NOT want to work for subsistence wages and in horrible conditions. So, no, I disagree with your statement about reality. We don't have equal opportunity. Clearly, inner-city kids have less opportunity.

DP: All minorities face discrimination, but they resolve that hurdle by hiring themselves, acquiring an education and acquiring a job skill. African and Latin-Americans, an aural culture living in an advanced industrialized economy, are at a disadvantage. Those from socially deprived families, not economically deprived, enter kindergarten with a 2,400 to 4,500 word-deficit increasing yearly. In other words, discrimination makes things harder, but does not explain a lower level of prosperity.

CVB: You clearly want to suggest, as most wealthy white Americans do, that it's only internal circumstances, like attitude, gratitude, drive, and grit, and NOT external circumstances, like culture, family, connections, inheritance, opportunity, that determine levels of prosperity. The well-to-do always underestimate external circumstances in favor of a better attitude. It's not an equal playing field.

DP: Immigrants come to this country precisely because the chance of success is higher here than anywhere else in the world.

CVB: Opportunity requires an even playing field. Otherwise, some people always lose, some always win. There has to be checks and balances, otherwise politicians will be bribed to favor the winners. The U.S. military-industrial complex is just that. Driven by profit, they influence policy such that government purchases more arms. It's why the U.S. pays for all of NATO while Europe pays almost nothing—guaranteed arms sales. It's why we support Israel—guaranteed arms sales. Profit! Like private prisons—policy with the wrong incentive tilts the playing field in favor of the wealthy.

DP: The U.S. pays for and supplies almost all of NATO because our military is infinitely more advanced. Europe allows this because it trusts the U.S. Europe starts wars, the U.S. stops them. Europe and the UN watched Serbs massacre citizens of Bosnia until President Clinton couldn't take it any longer and sent in American troops. Europe allows America to pay for NATO because that's the only way European socialism can afford universal healthcare and luxurious pensions. They pay nothing for their own defense.

CVB: Government intervention, rules, is what keeps others from tilting the playing field, from gaming the system. Professional football is the perfect analogy. Each year the winning NFL team picks new draftees last, whereas the losing team picks first—to keep the playing field level such that over the years all teams have a chance of winning—so that fans keep coming back, which they won't if their home team never wins, or, which is the same thing, the same teams keep winning year after year.

DP: NFL football is not the perfect analogy. NFL football is a market response to a market problem, a perfect analogy for how the market works without government intervention. And then, government can't regulate, create rules, such as antitrust or anti-insider trading legislation. It's not possible to tell if a given business practice is competitive or anti-competitive. With regulation of Google about to happen [2021], the risk is that antitrust legislation will prevent a superior market response. With new and complicated industries, business decisions are often enigmatic to outsiders, and perhaps only partially understood by the innovators themselves. The cost of regulation is that it deters innovation. Government has no business picking and choosing winners in the market. Creative destruction guarantees that all firms die. Three out of one hundred of the nation's top firms on the Dow Jones Industrial Average in 1961 are there today. Fifty years from now people will ask, "What's Facebook?"

CVB: Democracy needs constant defending too.

[We agree.]

DP: Government shouldn't subsidize business.

[We agree.]

CVB: Because corporations are legally considered persons, that allows them to contribute as much as they want to political parties as an expression of free speech. That allows politicians to be bribed—legalized bribery.

[We agree.]

DP: But it's a market problem for the market to solve.

CVB: The profit motive is an incentive for corporations to sacrifice safety for profit. It's human nature. It cannot be avoided.

DP: Not if there is competition.

[We agree.]

CVB: BUT WE DON'T HAVE COMPETITION! Government must intervene to enforce rules that prevent profit-incentivized firms from hurting society. For example, the security on the Texas-East Coast oil pipeline was hacked because owners cut costs that would have prevented that—just to increase profit.

[Agreed]

DP: I don't believe we need government to create and enforce rules. The market does that naturally.

CVB: Take money out of politics, and I might agree with you. But lawmakers are bribed to make laws that create artificial unfairness IN THE MARKET such that it cannot do that naturally, as you are suggesting.

DP: You can't. Illegal money will take over, politics will become a black-market operation. Bad policy.

CVB: Technology can monitor and enforce.

DP: Markets can monitor and enforce. Or, let a neutral third party, not necessarily government, monitor and enforce. Example— Department of Building Inspection, DBI, in San Francisco authorizes private engineering firms to monitor the placement of steel rebar before concrete is poured for building foundations.

CVB: That is subject to corruption. Business is just as corrupt as government, maybe more so.

DP: No, engineering is a competitive profession. Those engineers approved by the DBI are lucky. They will do nothing careless or corrupt. They risk losing that money-making privilege.

CVB: The military needs to be a function of government.

DP: A private party, the Taliban, defeated the U.S. in Afghanistan.

CVB: We lost because we knew we couldn't win, actually years ago, but we stayed in because the military-industrial complex profit motive pushed government to purchase arms. We created a kleptocracy instead of a government. The profit motive did that.

DP: No. We were in Vietnam, Iraq, Afghanistan for the wrong reasons—to build a better society, to stop the spread of communism, to protect oil—but not to make a profit.

CVB: We support Israel because they buy our arms.

DP: Either we fight the Palestinians, a terrorist organization, or Israel fights them. If Israel loses, all of Israel will have to move to New York City.

DP: Our disagreement is timeless. Classical liberal versus romantic liberal, reason, Apollo versus heart, Dionysus. Neither has one hundred percent of the answer.

CVB: Those terms sound like older people versus younger people. Conservative versus liberal. It's better to say one is socially liberal but economically conservative, thus, conservative, Or that one is socially liberal but also economically liberal, thus, progressive. I AM a capitalist, but I believe the system needs fixing. The market is rigged. it's not a level playing field. it needs regulation.

[Agreed.]

DP: But government can't solve that problem.

CVB: Then a neutral third party to monitor.

[Agreed.]

DP: That neutral third party also needs monitoring. That is the checks and balances that Madison created in the Constitution and described in *Federalist 51*. Why, then, does Congress pass off its legislating power to government administrative agencies, the EPA, for example? Because politicians are afraid of doing something or voting for something that later makes them unelectable. That's an incorrect use of government as a neutral third party.

CVB: Because the market bribes politicians not to enforce the law. The profit motive pushes manufacturers to dump trash into the river. The laws that politicians enforce or do not enforce are not governed by what the people want but by what corporations want.

DP: If you believe that, you have no faith in the people. You don't believe in democracy.

CVB: No, I believe in the people. What I don't believe is that the elite—the wealthy, the powerful—will ever play fair and not CHEAT the system for their own benefit because they can. I believe this will always happen when you let markets balance the culture and the economy without proper safety measures like well-enforced regulations, as well as some carefully chosen social spending. I believe in democracy. I just don't think we actually have it in the United States.

DP: We do. There are no advanced industrialized economies where the owners of capital don't have a strong say—except China—which also explains why the market is slow to respond to climate change. Heavily invested industrialists can't just toss in the towel.

CVB: With Covid-19, the economy shrank, but pollution also went way down. The earth healed beyond what anyone would have expected.

DP: To clean up pollution, you can't just stop the economy. One, that will throw us back to the Middle Ages. Two, the damage has been done. The only solution now is to remove CO_2 from the atmosphere.

CBV: But letting the market, or even nature, balance itself out will require many lost lives before the balance completes itself. How many lost lives are acceptable to allow markets to respond in their own good time?

DP: China pollutes more than the U.S. THEIR response is that the U.S. and Europe polluted to build their industries and so will China —until we are as rich as you. Then, we will clean up, probably with nuclear energy.

CVB: I guess Mars exploration is a market phenomenon. Move to space rather than solve our problems.

DP: Let's accept some irony, some Zen reconciliation of opposites.

CVB: Rugged individualism.

DP: For rich and poor.

CVB: Agreed.

Conclusion

Why do I write? I write because I'm compelled to communicate an intuition for political economy, my warning to the world: reduce the size of government. Scholarly writing in political economy from an entrepreneurial mind. Rare.

I predicted these events:

2008—*At the start* of the financial crisis, I said recovery would take ten years, after which the world would experience ten years of low economic growth. Interest rates would remain low for 20 years.

2010—*At the start* of the euro crisis, when Greece defaulted on its sovereign debt, to disbelief, I declared there was no crisis. My argument: the euro never fell in value, not even at the moment of default.

2015—*At the moment* Donald Trump announced his candidacy for president, I announced, "He won!" Everyone laughed.

2016—On the eve of Trump's election, with all polls giving Clinton a wide margin of victory, some by as much as 90 percent, I declared without hesitation, "He won."

I continually state these underlying economic truths:

Rates of return on investment are timeless. True in Babylon, true today: 1-2 percent on savings; 2-3 percent on mortgage lending; 3-5 percent on venture capital (higher because risk is higher).

In a competitive economy, profit is zero. No benefit to overthrowing a free society to obtain ownership of the means of production: nothing to distribute.

You cannot tax the poor; they have no money. You cannot tax the rich; they won't give you their money. You can only tax the hard-working middle class; they have no idea how to get out of paying.

Because profit is zero, taxation and regulation of business have to be passed back to the population as higher prices. No net gain to the nation; business circumvents all regulation. The purpose of Wall Street.

Except, with taxation and regulation, only the very large corporations survive. Only they, with their low long-run average costs, i.e., economies of scale, can absorb the cost of compliance—but then immediately buy up their small- and medium-sized competition. That marks the beginning of the *corporate state*, where a nation's government protects its monopoly corporations in exchange for those corporations doing its bidding: pay high wages, high pensions, health care, education, and with those high wages, enable citizens to access their nation's culture—museums, concerts, fine restaurants—all in all, provide psychological freedom, with citizens no longer worrying about employment, about having enough money. It works wherever citizens are willing to give up political freedom, Germany, for example, in the 1930s. It's called national socialism, socialism from the right, fascism, the abbreviation of which is NAZI. From the left, it's called communism, Cuba, the one difference being that under communism, the state rather than a few monopolist corporations owns the means of production.

Except, the purpose of government is to protect, not provide life, liberty and property.

Why? Because social, political and economic freedom are so inherently interconnected that the degree to which society constrains one of those freedoms is the degree to which it constrains the other two. Citizens, don't cancel speech; don't cancel culture; don't regulate business. The market, nature itself, self-corrects without government intervention.

Society cannot solve social and economic problems via the political process. Government cannot solve citizens' personal problems. Money does not solve problems. If it could there would be no problems. Government cannot do for citizens what they must do for themselves, i.e., get up in the morning. Worse, government undermines self-reliance. Poverty was 15 percent in 1965. Fifty-five years and trillions of dollars later, still 15 percent. Money for public education doubled; test scores dropped 25 percent. The War on Poverty, throwing money, progressivism, solved nothing. "The last ask is the greatest treason. To do the right deed for the wrong reason." –T.S. Eliot. Helping people that society knows are not helping themselves by taxing the hardworking middle class is immoral.

Business cycles are a constant:

1. Other than from a natural catastrophe, an economic downturn is *always* the result of an overextension of credit. And always teaches the same lesson: citizens, expect it! Always have half a year's income in savings. Businesses, you fail for the same reason: you cannot hold on during a downturn.

2. Leveraged investment guarantees that an economy will crash. With the rate of return on a leveraged investment twice that of an all-cash investment, businesses that don't borrow, including banks, cannot compete with those that do—who with their profits doubled because of leverage lower their prices until they've eliminated the competition, the well-managed but unleveraged firm. Again, creation of the corporate state.

———

I'm compelled to write because I have an understanding of political economy based on 150 years' personal experience: 40 years an inner-city public school teacher (plus 10 years a volunteer); 40 years a professional musician (20 years Berkeley Symphony Orchestra; 20 years Dave Parker Sextet, which twice headlined San Francisco's Fillmore Jazz Festival); 50 years professional real estate investment (with assets over $100 million); 35 years reading and writing in political economy (35,000 hours). I know what I'm talking about.

Writers who describe the lives and work of successful persons in business but themselves are not in business do not know what the business-experienced person knows. I do. Andrew Carnegie, for example, an inspiration to this author, has been criticized for ruthlessly monopolizing the steel industry and exploiting labor. William Mulholland was criticized for ruthlessly purchasing land and water rights from Owens Valley to Los Angeles, then bringing water to a location where water would never go naturally, through a desert. Donald Trump was mocked for paying $1 million each for apartments worth $500,000 at Columbus Circle in New York City. All three, Carnegie, Mulholland, Trump, had the larger vision. All three knew the timing was right. All three had the ability to act fearlessly in starting and carrying out a risky project. Entrepreneurship. Andrew Carnegie did not monopolize steel by cutting prices to force out small companies. The steel mills and railroads (the main purchaser of steel) were interlocking directorates: they owned each other. They divided up sales according to how much they could produce. Neither the steel mills nor the railroads failed. Employees were not laid off. Carnegie said he was at the right place at the right time, Pittsburg 1870. And he was fearless in his relentless increasing of production right on through the Panic of 1873, when everyone else stopped, which allowed Carnegie to grab ever more market share (and keep his workers employed). See Chapter 4, "Gradually I Came to Appreciate Andrew Carnegie."

For William Mulholland, it was his unwavering knowledge that Los Angeles, population 102,000 in 1900, would one day be 15 million. For Trump, it was fearless acquisition of $1 million apartments (worth $500,000) that he knew would each be worth $10 million. Trump Tower.

All three exemplify individual leadership. All three had to overcome resistance, which is why conservatives regard the *individual* as the quintessential endangered minority. Conservatives trace individual rights to human nature—which has no race ethnicity, gender or class. Individual rights (Western civilization) imply freedom, although freedom implies inequality. There's no in-between: freedom or equality, capitalism or Marxism, not both. Choose!

I just don't understand. I leave my apartment on the Upper West Side in the morning, converse with people in the hallway, at cafés and stores downstairs, in the subway going to work in the Village, with people at work. Not one person said they voted for Bush. Who *are* these people?

—New York film critic Pauline Kael,
after George H.W. Bush won the presidency in 1988

Made in the USA
Middletown, DE
06 October 2022

11950710R00133